MYTHS, TALL TALES AND HALF TRUTHS OF CAPE COD

JAMES H. ELLIS

THE
History
PRESS

Published by The History Press
Charleston, SC
www.historypress.com

Copyright © 2023 by James H. Ellis
All rights reserved

First published 2023

Manufactured in the United States

ISBN 9781467154444

Library of Congress Control Number: 2023935536

For June

CONTENTS

PREFACE

I think we call a lot of things 'history' that aren't history. A lot of stuff that we call 'history' is really folklore, myth, or tourism," claims noted historian Jill Lepore.[1] There is much to her position, and it forms the theme of this book.

Stretching the truth about history is a trait with a broad reach. In this matter, the people of Cape Cod do not take a back seat to those in any region. Venerated institutions on the peninsula such as churches have little difficulty gilding the lily. And amazingly, the area's historical societies are practiced at the art. Embellishment and exaggeration come easily. Naturally, the Cape's sporting scene—from baseball to golf—is not left behind. Some stories seem too good to correct. In the end, the belief of the Harriet Beecher Stowe character who thought it advisable to "contrive allers [always] to keep just the happy medium between truth and falsehood" seems to govern.[2]

Occasionally called mytho-history, the practice takes several forms. Tall tales usually are obvious. Told for fun, they are meant to be enjoyed rather than believed. Boastfulness often stands out as such, and it is at the core of a fair amount of the misleading. A common boast on the Cape is the use of the term "wash ashore." Residents who are not natives place themselves in this imaginary category, suggesting the label is applied by natives to set them off as second-class new arrivals. This is not the case. These people invented the nom de guerre with a maritime tone to give themselves a sense of belonging to this special place, knowing full well they will never be true Cape Codders.

Insufficient research and analysis account for a great deal of the incorrectness. Misreading the facts is exceedingly common. The end results are indiscriminately and honestly repeated over and over, seeming to gain credibility with each telling. Much of it is innocent and, in the grand scheme of things, unimportant. Thus, most of the misinformation goes uncorrected. People, almost unknowingly, filter what they read and repeat, changing for their own needs. And when corrected, they respond in different ways. Many readily accept correction. But, almost humorously, some dig in and reject even the most compelling evidence of inaccuracy. Examples of both of these reactions will be presented in the succeeding pages.

The use of superlatives more often than not is a red flag. *Oldest, first, biggest, earliest* and similar tags are misapplied so often they always merit skepticism. Almost without fail, a challenger can be found. A few representative examples follow. Superlatives usually are employed for emphasis, not accuracy.

I am reminded of one of my early bosses. As a research associate with a public interest organization in Hartford, Connecticut, I conducted studies and wrote reports on public policy issues. Many of the topics were far-reaching and controversial. Accuracy and clarity were imperative. Moreover, government officials, the legislature, the media and the public at large expected consistent and careful truthfulness in our reports. Once I finished a draft, I sat before the research director, who went over the report. At every purported statement of fact, he looked up and asked, "Are you sure?" And that is the point. So many who seriously write or talk about the area's history are not sure of the facts. They pick up a scrap of misinformation along the way and instinctively accept it as authentic and certain. Repeated once again, it moves toward general acceptance.

During a lifetime as a history enthusiast, I have noted countless instances of incorrectness. A few Cape Cod examples will be treated after an inside look at the birth of a celebrated tall tale.

ACKNOWLEDGEMENTS

I am appreciative of the aid provided by the resources of the National Archives, Department of the Navy, Cape Cod National Seashore, American Film Institute, National Baseball Hall of Fame, Massachusetts Historical Society, Falmouth (MA) Historical Society, Historical Society of Old Yarmouth (MA), Stonington (CT) Historical Society, Cape Cod Community College Library, Centerville (MA) Library, Sturgis of Barnstable (MA) Library, Yarmouth Port (MA) Library, Camden Public Library (ME) and the Newington (NH) Town Administrator's Office.

Also, I am especially grateful for the help of Rebekah Ambrose-Dalton, Michael Bertucci, Bill Burke, Jennifer Burke, Tom Colombo, Lynn Comandich, Lucy Loomis, Chelsea Mitchell and Marie Kesten Zahn.

And then there is June Bertucci. For some years, this book rattled around in my head. It took June to spring it loose. Her interest and soft encouragement followed by extensive assistance made the writing easy. Simply put, if June had not crossed my path, this book would not have been written.

CHAPTER 1

THE ORIGIN
OF THE DOUGHNUT HOLE

T he origins of most familiar tall tales are uncertain. Repeated and embellished over the years, they take on a life of their own, and authorship becomes unknown and unimportant. Nonetheless, one may wonder what prompted a particular fanciful and hard-to-believe story. What is behind the tale? In the case of a celebrated Cape Cod fantasy, with inside information, these details can be revealed.

In July 1941, the *Portland Telegram* reported on the plans of Camden, Maine, to erect a statue in memory of a local sea captain credited with inventing the hole in the doughnut in 1847. Fried dough in some form has been around since ancient Rome. But the Camden Chamber of Commerce asserted it took a Mainer almost two centuries ago to come up with the hole in the delicacy.

The newspaper report indicated a young Hanson Crockett Gregory asked his mother to make her doughnuts with holes in the middle, thereby eliminating soggy centers. This account did not excite much interest. If anything, the story promoted doubt. Embellishment followed. The first revision indicated Captain Gregory, years later, reacted to the near drowning of a crewman overboard. Usually skilled at swimming, the man struggled in the water due to a belly full of heavy johnnycakes. Gregory assessed the situation, picked up a belaying pin and punched a hole in the remaining cakes. Etymologists, it is said, trace the slang word *sinkers* to the incident.

But this explanation still seemed unconvincing. A less dramatic account followed. Gregory, intent on keeping his helmsmen at the wheel at all times, simply instructed them to stick their fried cakes on the spokes of the ship's wheel, putting them within ready grasp. And the hole in the doughnut became common along shore Down East and beyond.

When the *Telegram* report appeared, Alton H. "Blackie" Blackington from the North Shore of Boston was visiting my grandfather Henry A. Ellis, a prominent Hyannis lawyer. The Maine tale was right in Blackie's wheelhouse. A veteran Boston newspaperman, with notebook and camera in hand, he spent years roaming New England chronicling the region's legends and lore. By the early '50s, he had a popular NBC radio show called *Yankee Yarns*, later moving it to television. And he put his best stories in two books: *Yankee Yarns* and *More Yankee Yarns*.

After reading the Maine story, "Blackie" set the newspaper down and queried, "We can do better than that, can't we, Henry?" And of course, they could. Both men knew how to trifle with the Maine psyche. Blackington was born and grew up in Rockland, Maine, residing outside of town on West Meadow Road. And Ellis graduated from the University of Maine Law School in Orono.

They would not be alone. An East Dorset, Vermont man sent a note to *Yankee* magazine asserting his grandfather Shadrach Gowallapus Hooper deserved the credit for coming up with the hole in the doughnut. Not to be outdone, New Hampshire came forth with the claim a Granite State woodsman thought of the idea. The governor of Maine, feigning shock, demanded the New Hampshire governor take back his state's outrageous assertion or else.

The better tall tales center on a real person, thereby lending a touch of credibility. The two men on a quiet Sunday morning in Hyannis decided to feature Henry's grandmother—Sally Greenough Cobb.

Sally Greenough Cobb (1817–1904). *Private collection.*

In 1859, the Massachusetts legislature enacted a measure calling for the study of the social situation of Massachusetts Indians. A Worcester newspaper publisher and politician, John M. Earle, received the assignment. Although it is not a census, many treat the resulting report as such. Known as the 1861 *Earle Report*, its appendix names the 1,448 "Indians" found in the state. Sally Cobb, age forty-two, is listed as a member of the Yarmouth band, as she was in the earlier *Briggs Report*. Her daughter, Sarah Eliza Cobb, age three, also appears. Sally, granddaughter of Thomas Greenough, a noted Cape Indian in his day, was Henry's grandmother. This was the only fact the pair needed to weave an entertaining challenge to the Maine claim.

Born in 1747, Thomas Greenough amassed a fair amount of property in Yarmouth and became influential in the town's affairs. "Endowed with an uncommon share of penetration and capable of a just appreciation of rights, he wore, through the last year of his life, the title of 'Lawyer.'" He died at age ninety, and the local newspaper recalled, "He displayed in the management of the business, such tact and skill as few of more pretensions or statesmanship would have blushed to own."[3] The national *Niles' Weekly Register* considered him important enough to carry his obituary under the heading "The Last of the Nobscussets."[4] Tradition suggests he was the model for John Greenleaf Whittier's poem "Nauhaught, the Deacon."

Returning to 1941, by mid-August, the Cape Cod response had appeared in the *Boston Sunday Herald*. In the first years of English settlement on Cape Cod, it was said, a Puritan woman was cooking johnnycakes outside in a large kettle. Two Nobscusset hunters came upon the scene at a distance. The cakes appeared enticing. The pair calculated if they shot an arrow at the kettle, it would scare the woman away long enough to allow them to run up and grab some of the cooking. But the arrow came in high. Instead of clanging off the kettle, the arrow pierced a johnnycake just as the cook prepared to place it in the steaming vat. She screamed bloody murder and accidentally dropped the cake into the kettle before retreating. The unexpected commotion rattled the two hunters. They skulked away deeper into the woods. Moments later, the lady came out of her cabin to find the first doughnut with a hole in its center.

Many years later, a young Henry sat in Grandmother Sally's lap as she told him how their ancestors had a hand in creating the first doughnut hole.

Maine wasted little time before responding to the insult. Betty Foxwell, secretary of the Camden Chamber of Commerce, telegraphed Ellis that Maine sea captains "will sail on Hyannis unless story publicly retracted."[5] At the same time, she thanked "Blackie" for keeping the "doughnut kettle boiling."[6] Blackie had just placed the story in the *Christian Science Monitor*. Ellis replied to Foxwell, "Being a lawyer my devotion to the truth is so intense that I am unable to retract my statement." He added, "Before you sail, I want to remind you…the neighboring town of Mashpee is entirely populated by Indians who would undoubtedly stand by a tribesman in distress." He also suggested she "go up to Old Town and learn the Indian sign of peace." He assured her, "If you come bearing the Indian sign of peace, I would be glad to confer with you."[7]

An arrow pierces a johnnycake, creating the hole in the doughnut. *Private collection.*

Blackington could not resist getting into the exchange. He teased Foxwell, telling her Ellis had amassed "an amazing amount" of supporting material. In fact, he has even produced a "High Medicine Man of his tribe—a real honest-to-God full-blooded Indian with great dignity and lots of feathers and facts."[8]

Foxwell retorted, describing herself as a "widow with ten children and tipping the scales at 309 pounds." She bragged, "I am a match for any of your Cape Cod Indians."[9]

Behind the scenes, more letters were exchanged. Ellis got back to Foxwell: "It is generally assumed that Lawyers are the biggest liars in the world, but it seems to me they are fairly matched by Secretaries of Chambers of Commerce." He referred to her claim to weigh over three hundred pounds: "Blackington was down Sunday and showed me your picture. My greatest regret is that I am 62 years old."[10]

The wire services and newspapers all over the country jumped on the story. Over one thousand papers copied Blackington's full-length version that appeared in the *Boston Sunday Herald* on August 24, 1941. A Los Angeles Chinese paper sent Ellis a copy of one of their editions said to include the doughnut hole story. "Perhaps it did," he mused.[11] And the Pillsbury Cooking School in Minneapolis, Minnesota, sent him a large doughnut, claiming the Indian method was used to make the hole.

The National Dunking Association in New York, an offshoot of the Doughnut Corporation of America, saw its opportunity and took it. They began by giving Blackington the Grand Llama of the Dunk award. Only the third person to be so honored, he joined Virginia congressman Jennings Randolph and actor John Barrymore. Mainers thought he should have received the Grand Llama of Bunk honor. Actually, it became clear some in the Pine Tree State were truly upset.

But the honorary for "Blackie" wasn't enough. The association pushed for an early November national radio debate to be held in the Hotel Astor in New York City. Both sides accepted. Camden enlisted local Fred Crockett, a distant relative of Captain Gregory, to represent Maine. Ellis brought along Mashpee Wampanoag chief High Eagle (William James) to buttress his case.

Journalist Franklin Adams, intellectual and author Clifton Fadiman and gossip columnist Elsa Maxwell served as judges. By all accounts, James, in full regalia, stole the show. However, it all fell short. The panel ruled in favor of the Maine claim. The Cape felt the decision was tainted since members of the jury summered in Maine. Crockett reported to Foxwell: "Ellis sure knows how to speak in an eloquent way." He admitted, "I was sort of scared…. Many a jury has been swayed on much less facts than what he had."[12]

In an amusing turn of events, not too many years later, Crockett became the executive of the Cape Cod Boy Scout Council. As such, he held sway over Camp Greenough in Yarmouth Port. The camp's name traces to Thomas Greenough, onetime owner of the land.

My grandfather continued to have fun with his story, presenting his case, for example, to the Camp Edwards doughboys during the war. In a later year, he confessed, "I have told this story so many times that I believe it."[13]

And this is a point central to so many of the myths and misrepresentations that follow. An erroneous story, claim or tale is repeated so often and for so long that eventually it becomes accepted as fact. Oldest this or that claims are quite susceptible to this outcome.

CHAPTER 2

OLDEST IN THE COUNTRY

T is a rule of manners to avoid exaggeration," thought essayist Ralph Waldo Emerson.[14] But when it comes to matters of history, some on Cape Cod have forgotten their manners. Their use of superlatives in such situations often leads to overstatements. When something is acclaimed *oldest* or *first* of its kind, beware. A review of the facts as often as not will find overstepping the bounds of truth. Buildings are favorite subjects of such treatment.

In 1627, the leaders of Plymouth Plantation moved to improve their trade capabilities. In addition to the continuing need for provisions and the like, the settlers strived to disengage themselves of the substantial debt they owed their sponsors back in England. They built a little vessel known as a pinnace at the head of what is now called Buzzards Bay. Locating their boat at this place twenty miles overland from Plymouth and on the other side of an isthmus enabled them to carry on trade to the south with the Dutch and Indigenous peoples without the need of "compassing of Cape Cod, and those dangerous shoals."[15] The *Mayflower* almost perished in those hazardous waters as it approached landfall in 1620. They also constructed a house at this spot—to be known as the Aptucxet trading post. A pair of agents managed the property. Aptucxet in the Native language means "little trap in the river." In this case, the river close by the post was the Manomet, sometimes called the Monument.

The building had been used for as little as two years before the great hurricane of 1635 destroyed it, blowing off the roof and leaving only the posts. There is a belief Plymouth leadership replaced the structure, but

Aptucxet Trading Post. *J.H. Ellis.*

Craig Chartier and R.A. Lovell say it was not rebuilt. There is an indication the Pilgrims had abandoned the place at a time well before the storm. At any rate, its exact siting as suggested by the replica is open to question. A second excavation of the presumed spot took place in 1926, followed by the erection of the present replica and museum at that location in Bourne village. The selected spot proved to be the location of an early dwelling, not the trading post. The precise site of the post may have been disturbed and effectively lost during the 1914 construction of the Cape Cod Canal.

Being a tourist attraction, it is no surprise Aptucxet is shrouded in exaggeration. The Bourne Historical Society's website claims Aptucxet "became the first private commercial enterprise using a local currency known as wampum," or the little cylindrical beads made of shells from quahogs and like shellfish. This prompted the local daily newspaper to describe Aptucxet as "America's Cradle of Commerce."[16] Others made similar pronouncements. Betsey D. Keene called it "the first place of organized business in New England, and perhaps the first in this Country."[17] Chartier views it differently. The replica and its supposed underlying history became a symbol to townspeople. "Plymouth was the Foundation of American Democracy…but here in Bourne was the Foundation of American Commerce." He added: "Visit Plymouth, and then come to Bourne and hear the rest of the story, and while you're here, shop and spend."[18]

The facts show Isaack de Rasieres, head trader for the Dutch at Fort Amsterdam (present-day New York City), introduced wampum to the Plymouth traders while on a visit to Aptucxet. In 1614, the Dutch also erected a trading post known as Fort Nassau at the locale of what is now Albany. A decade later, they added a second post nearby named Fort Orange. The Dutch, Rasieres explained, used wampum at these facilities to buy furs from the Native trappers about the Hudson River. Plymouth hesitated to accept the concept but adopted the measure before long. And wampum proved so popular with the region's Natives that Plymouth for a time monopolized the New England fur trade.

The truth of the matter shows Europeans began trading as soon as they arrived on the continent. Giovanni da Verrazano (1524), Bartholomew Gosnold (1602), George Weymouth (1605) and John Smith (1614) all traded with the Indigenous peoples. In the 1604–6 period, Pierre Dugua Sieur de Mons set up French trading posts at and about Clarks Point, Machiasport and Cross Island, Cutler in present-day Maine. The better-known royal cartographer Samuel de Champlain traveled under Dugua. In the next decade, in 1613, Claude de Saint-Etienne de la Tour established a trading post and fishing terminal known as Fort Pentagouet in what is now Castine, Maine. This became the first permanent settlement in the present six-state region of New England. In addition, Samuel Eliot Morison notes Jamestown, Virginia, started as a trading post in 1607. In fact, Plymouth began trading immediately, long before Aptucxet. So, organized commerce existed elsewhere in the colonies much before Aptucxet. Claiming earliest for the Bourne trading post, therefore, is more than a stretch.

Eighteenth-century residential houses on the Cape seem to attract an inordinate amount of misrepresentation. Almost every neighborhood in the areas initially settled near and along the shores, it seems, has at least one old house said to go back to the First Period (before 1725). Noted architectural historian Abbott Lowell Cummings thought there are "a surprisingly large number of houses in Massachusetts which have been advertised as earlier than they actually are." Cummings explained that over the years, "the average lay person and many historians as well had tended to assign earlier dates than were justified to a significantly large number of houses" from the first one hundred years of the state's settlement.[19]

Not too many years ago, a property in Barnstable village along the Old King's Highway went on the market masquerading as a 1640 dwelling. History buffs scoffed at the claim, knowing homes of that date were humble, hastily built structures, little more than hovels. The place in question was a relatively substantial more modern property. Architectural historian Fisk Kimball warned "against acceptance of dates…which prove little more than that there was a dwelling house on a given site in early years." He stressed, "Any dates prior to 1650 must be advanced with extreme caution."[20]

And this proved to be the case with the Barnstable home. In the first years of the town's settlement, a structure was situated on the footprint of the house for sale. The town assessor changed the property's records to show a construction date of 1740, more in keeping with the building's possible age. The relatively prompt correction of the record appears unusual. "Even the most authoritative documentation has seldom succeeded in changing many minds," observed Cummings.[21] There is a certain romance to being able to say your house traces to the 1600s.

Rather than reviewing more Cape homes with questionable if not doubtful claims of First Period construction, it will better serve to note a building with a proven record of colonial beginnings. Such a discussion will show the extensive processes necessary to validate such claims. And the undoubted costs for a professional study demonstrate why very few claimants have elected to go this route. Instead, they turn to handed-down beliefs, customs and legends from generations past. But tradition has proven time and again to be a most unreliable authority.

The building is the Sturgis Library in the village of Barnstable, long advertised as the "oldest library building in the United States." In particular, reference is made to the southeast corner of the obviously old three-story house that fronts the street and is separable from the adjoining modern complex. This stately structure encompasses a single-story two-room dwelling erected in 1644 as the second home of Reverend John Lothrop, the minister and leader of Barnstable's settlement. Simply, addition upon addition, while retaining the old home, resulted in an overall building appearing at first blush to be of a much later period. Nonetheless, a 2014 professional study settled the question.

For years, the best evidence pointing to the age of the southeastern section of the building involved observations made during routine repairs and additions and the writing of Amos Otis (1801–1875). Otis (we will hear much more from him later) was a renowned Cape historian and genealogist. Charles F. Swift, another acclaimed local historian, said of the works of Otis: "They will always be referred to as authority on the points which they discuss."[22] And Otis, in his genealogy of Lothrop, offers a fairly detailed description of the old place.

"Mr. Lothrop's new house was 21 feet on the front or south side and 29 feet on the east side. The chimney was on the west side."[23] Otis went on to describe the front posts, sills, floors, framing and height of beams. He also

Sturgis Library, Barnstable, Massachusetts. *J.H. Ellis.*

sited the building, discussed four early additions and treated the description of the house in Lothrop's will.

All of this matched the twenty-first-century reality. But in a sense, it was not enough. The library board of trustees commissioned a 2014 professional study of the issue. The study team led by Hadley Crow Studio from Providence, Rhode Island, included an architect, two archaeologists, a structural engineer, two area practitioners of restoration, a building contractor and a window restoration specialist. As well, the team retained the services of the Oxford Dendrochronology Laboratory in South Oxfordshire, England.

While so much of the old house is associated with Reverend Lothrop, it came to the town as an 1863 bequest of Captain William F. Sturgis. He also left $15,000 to support a library in the building. Sturgis was born in the place in 1782, and he purchased it shortly before his death in 1863. One of the great men of the town, Sturgis, like so many Cape Cod boys of his era, went to sea at a young age. He became a leading Boston merchant after joining John Bryant in 1810 to form the Bryant & Sturgis firm. Together, they made fortunes in the Northwest Coast fur trade, California hides trade and China trade. Highly regarded, Sturgis represented Boston in the Massachusetts House of Representatives and Senate, serving for over thirty years.

The most significant findings of the team involved dendrochronology—the dating of archaeological artifacts by measuring and analyzing annual growth rings in timber and tree trunks. The science of dendrochronology is based on biology and statistics. Measurements are compared against dated reference chronologies. Analysis of two structural beams found one dated to a tree-felling in 1692–93. The other came from some date after 1673. A third timber proved unsuitable for testing due to advanced deterioration.

The 1692–93 beam certainly was placed to support the addition of the second floor "at a date after the original house was constructed." And the 1673 beam matched "known chronology of occupancy and expansion of original structure."[24] This phase of the overall study concluded: "In order to maintain skepticism" about the 1644 date of origin, one must assert the house bequeathed by Lothrop in 1653 was not the present structure. "Such a claim flies in the face of all the evidence gathered here and accumulated over the past three and one-half centuries."[25]

Otis made much the same point. "That the house now known as the Sturgis Library building was the new house named in Mr. Lothrop's will and built about the year 1644, hardly admits of doubt."[26]

Thus, the case for 1644 construction of the southeastern section of the house gifted by Sturgis is affirmed. But then the library management goes

Above: Lothrop room in Sturgis Library, the core of the 1644 house. *J.H. Ellis*.

Opposite: Sturgis chimney showing First Period construction. *J.H. Ellis*.

a little too far. The additional claim is made that the Lothrop section is "the oldest structure still standing in America where religious services were regularly held."[27] True, Lothrop built his larger second house in part to accommodate his flock. However, the San Jose Church, San Juan, Puerto Rico (1530); Cathedral of San Juan Bautista, San Juan, Puerto Rico (1540); San Miguel Mission, Santa Fe, New Mexico (1610s); and St. Luke's Church, Jamestown, Virginia (1632), all are older and beat out Sturgis.

While on the topic of religious buildings, it is noteworthy that houses of worship in New England seem to draw claims of venerated age. Cape Cod buildings are in the mix. The old "White Church" in West Barnstable, also known as the West Parish meetinghouse, is a prime example. For years, it has been plugged as "the oldest Congregational Church building in the United States."[28] But what does the record show?

Settled in 1638 and incorporated a year later, Barnstable is one of the largest towns in Massachusetts. It is made up of just under sixty square miles of land area in the mid-Cape. Consisting of one parish at the outset, by the second decade of the eighteenth century, the inhabitants felt time had arrived to split the town on a north–south line and add a second parish. Original settlement took place in the northeastern section of the town and eventually spread throughout to the south and west. Overwhelming support led to a 1717 division and a West Parish alongside an East Parish.

Immediately, the western parish bent to the task of building a meetinghouse. A three-man committee determined to site the building on a little knoll owned by John Crocker. Workers harvested local wood and fashioned it into lumber and timbers. After two years of labor, on Thanksgiving Day 1719, the initial service took place in the new meetinghouse.

Within four years, the place proved to be too small. So, parishioners pulled the building apart enough to join the two sections with another twenty feet of structure in the middle. In 1723, they built a tower on the north end. A total remodeling followed in 1852, achieving a Neoclassic appearance.

As early as 1922, with the meetinghouse in unhappy condition and the congregation consisting of a meager number of villagers, interest surfaced

1717 Meetinghouse, West Barnstable, Massachusetts. *J.H. Ellis.*

for a complete restoration going back to the 1723 model. Funding, of course, amounted to a seemingly overwhelming obstacle. Beginning in 1930, the first Sunday in August celebrated and honored the first pastor of the supposedly original fellowship in England. Henry Jacob Sunday became a means to generate enthusiasm outside of the village for the major undertaking. Eventually, in 1949, a West Parish Memorial Foundation gained incorporation and started to lead the fundraising and restoration effort. Work got underway in 1953, and by the middle of 1956, enough of the work was completed to permit services to resume in the building.

The Memorial Foundation has taken the new name of 1717 Meetinghouse Foundation. Completely separate from the West Parish Church society, its mission remains the same—to preserve and maintain the historic structure. Recently, the foundation undertook the significant and major task of restoring the half-ton bell in the meetinghouse tower. An original Revere bell installed in 1808 in memory of Colonel James Otis, the patriarch of the famous local family, cracked in 1833. A replacement Revere company bell went up but required attention by 2015. The foundation sent the bell to Ohio for necessary repairs. Over the years, the bell has sounded on special occasions as well as on its regular weekly basis. On April 19, 1951, for instance, it joined the chorus of numerous Revere bells pealing throughout New England celebrating Patriot's Day.

By tracing the origin to 1717, the year construction began, proponents gain a two-year lead in the aging game. Workers, as we have seen, completed the building, and occupancy took place in 1719. Thus, 1719 can be considered a more exact date of when the building came into existence. The two dates, however, are indisputable. This is not always the case when dates are assigned to subjects from the distant past.

One does not have to travel far to encounter a competing claim for the oldest Congregational church building. For some time, friends of the Old Indian Meeting House to the west in Mashpee have asserted their structure went up in 1684. The date is repeated often, even by authorities such as Sinnott. And though no longer the case, Congregationalism was the sole practice at the outset in Mashpee.

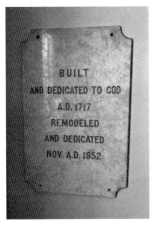

Marble plaque in tower room of 1717 Meetinghouse. *J.H. Ellis.*

Tradition indicates, beginning in 1637, the Mashpee Indians worshipped under a great oak at Briant's Neck jutting into Santuit Pond. A pair of white men, Richard Bourne and Thomas Tupper of Sandwich, guided the so-called Praying Indians. In 1684, the congregation erected a little meetinghouse nearby. The location was not close to the center of Mashpee, but it may have accommodated the two preachers from adjoining Sandwich. Purportedly, in 1717, the members moved the building a few miles to the southwest next to what is now known as the Old Indian Burying Ground close by the Mashpee River. There, a renovated structure stands today.

As so often is the case, the early year is questioned. A longtime member of the Mashpee Historical Commission, after lengthy study of written records, believes the present meetinghouse was built in 1758 at its current location. Rosemary Love Burns checked material at the Massachusetts State Archives, Massachusetts State House Library, Massachusetts Historical Society, Harvard University Library and the Rhodes Library at Oxford University, among other sources, before reaching her conclusion. Her opinion does not sit well with traditionalists.

The National Register of Historic Places does not settle the matter. Straddling the controversy, the Register presents both dates but appears to lean toward 1758. When adding a place to the Register, it must be noted, the National Park Service, the agency maintaining the listings, does not independently authenticate information submitted by an applicant. Verification is the responsibility of a State Historic Preservation Office, in this state a unit under the Massachusetts Historical Commission. In reality, submissions valid on their face are accepted.

This being said, a clear and substantive error in the designation undercuts the 1684 claim.

The Register reports Deacon John Hinckley built the structure in that year. But turning again to that man Otis, we find Hinckley was not born until 1701. A carpenter by trade, he served as a deacon in Barnstable's East Parish. He built throughout the town and beyond, and in 1762, he added the high steeple to the East Parish meetinghouse. Hinckley served as captain of the troop of horse in Barnstable County's First Regiment during the French and Indian War. To the issue at hand, in Hinckley's papers there is an October 4, 1757 letter from a Thomas Hubbard of Boston. Hubbard, a wealthy businessman, had a notable career, serving as speaker of the Massachusetts House of Representatives, treasurer of Harvard College, commissary general of the Province of Massachusetts Bay, deacon of the Old South Church and, significantly, an organizer for the Massachusetts Society for Propagating Christian Knowledge among the Indians of North America. Hinckley naturally turned to this man for help with his Mashpee project. In his letter, Hubbard advises he has bought ten thousand feet of "seasoned boards, and 16 m of good shingles for the Meeting House at Marshpee [sic], to be landed at Barnstable." From this and other Hinckley documentation, Otis declares, "He built the Meetinghouse at Mashpee in 1757 [OS]."[29] This plausible and persuasive evidence must be overcome before the 1758 date can be rejected and the 1684 date is accepted.

Now comes the Reverend Gideon Hawley. Shortly after graduating from Yale, he took a position with the Society for Propagating the Gospel among the

Old Indian Meeting House, Mashpee, Massachusetts. *J.H. Ellis.*

Indians teaching the Oneida and Mohawk tribes. Later, the commissioners of Indian Affairs sent him to set up a mission for the Six Nations in New York. The French and Indian War forced an end to the work. Hawley drifted to Boston and joined the militia as a chaplain. After his service, he pressed to get back into missionary work. New York remained too dangerous, so the society sent him to Mashpee. He took up this Cape post in April 1758. "I visited in their several little villages," he said, "and preached to them. At that time there were several churches altogether of Christian Indians, in this quarter, viz. one at Marshpee, one at Herring Pond…and down the county of Barnstable as far as Chatham was another very respectable church."[30] In reviewing Hawley's extensive and difficult-to-read journals and letter books, Burns found him mentioning he went to Mashpee with authorization to site a new meetinghouse. A year later, in March 1759, Hawley was thanking the commissioners for agreeing to lathe and plaster the building.

John Warren Barber's *Historical Collection* buttresses the assertion that Hawley initiated the construction of the present building. "The following cut [illustration] represents the Indian church," says Barber, "built under the direction of the Rev. Mr. Hawley, the missionary....It stands a short distance from the main road." He adds, "The Indian grave-yard is by the side of their church."[31] The illustration is a fair depiction of the present meetinghouse. And a main road and graveyard abut the existing structure.

The connections between Hinckley, Hubbard and Hawley are obvious. And their collective testimony leading to and supporting a 1758 construction date for the present Old Indian Meeting House is difficult to dismiss.

Nonetheless, a spokesman for the Mashpee Wampanoag Tribal Council declined to discuss the matter. He simply expressed confidence in the accuracy and validity of the 1684 construction date.

Leaving Mashpee and returning to West Barnstable and the 1717 Meetinghouse, a more credible challenge to its "oldest" claim exists. Moving north to Newington, New Hampshire, outside Portsmouth, one will find another old white meetinghouse from the past. The history of the town by Frederick M. Pickering and John F. Rowe states construction of this meetinghouse started in 1712 followed by occupancy two years later. "The building still stands on its original site and is considered the oldest structure in the country still in continuous use by Congregationalists."[32]

The ancient meetinghouse even antecedes the town by a year. During the early years of settlement, both Dover and Portsmouth claimed the area situated on a peninsula bordered by the Piscataquis River and Great Bay. After years of contention, the two towns met on the ground to settle ownership. Attendees became belligerent. Tempers flared, and swords were displayed. Cooler heads prevailed, however, avoiding bloodshed. The ownership question remained unresolved, but the village for a time gained the name of Bloody Point.

As years passed, inhabitants tired of struggling to negotiate the tides and currents in order to attend town meetings or religious services in either Dover or Portsmouth. As a consequence, in the early 1700s, Bloody Point became a separate parish. As such, a meetinghouse and church with a settled minister became a requirement. Work on the meetinghouse commenced in 1712. The town incorporated a year later, taking the name Newington from the English hamlet that donated a bell for the new meetinghouse. The first service took place in an unfinished building in 1713. As in West Barnstable, construction took two years. This record makes the Newington meetinghouse five years older than the West Barnstable structure. The original design followed the Federal style. An 1838 renovation converted the building to its present Greek Revival model.

Right: Old Indian
Meeting House
showing graveyard
described by John
Warren Barber. *J.H.
Ellis*.

Below: Newington,
New Hampshire Town
Church. *Jennifer Burke*.

THE PEOPLE OF NEWINGTON
AFTER BUILDING
THEIR MEETING HOUSE
IN 1712 – 13
AIDED BY THIRTEEN YOKE OF OXEN
MOVED FROM A FIELD OPPOSITE
THIS STONE, TO BE USED AS
THE TOWN HORSE BLOCK

A horse block with a plaque in front of Newington Church. *Jennifer Burke.*

After almost a century, in 1803, lightning struck and cracked the meetinghouse bell. With an ox team, the town's selectmen dragged the damaged bell to Boston, hoping Paul Revere could make repairs. Instead, he offered a deal. Revere had cast a bell for Pembroke, Massachusetts, that turned out to be too small for that town's needs. But the surplus bell proved the perfect size for Newington. In exchange for their damaged bell and $210, the Newington selectmen returned home with the Pembroke bell. The bell continues to peal to this day. As well, the old meetinghouse displays Revere's 1804 handwritten bill of sale, a special memento.

In 2012, the town celebrated its meetinghouse's 300th anniversary. The Newington church society is modest, and their claim is not widely known. However, their situation appears incontrovertible and reduces the West Parish to no better than second place in the oldest Congregational church building in the country discussion. But there always is an oldest in the world category.

CHAPTER 3

OLDEST IN THE WORLD

Traveling through New England, one will come across an oldest-in-the-country boast sprouting up in what seems to be every town. There is the oldest family farm and the first clam shack. You may find the original cranberry bog. But first or oldest in the world usually is a bridge too far for local pride. However, we do not have to leave the West Parish to find such an exaggeration.

Since the mid-1800s, the church society that worships in West Barnstable's 1717 meetinghouse has claimed to be the very same fellowship that gathered in 1616 in the Southwark section of London, England. Asserting an unbroken existence since, in a brief history, it is declared, "In the year 1616, *this church* [emphasis added] was organized in the City of London, England, by Rev. Henry Jacob. Thus, the foundation was laid of the First Independent Congregational Church, by that name, in England."[33] The *Boston Recorder*, a Congregationalist weekly newspaper established in 1816, traces the origin of the claim to Reverend Enoch Pratt. The January 26, 1838 issue notes that when he left the pastorate in 1835, he wrote and lectured about the church's history and made the originality assertion. As well as in writings, throughout the years, the church has advanced the claim on banners, posters and signs. Authoritative sources have accepted the story without question and repeat the belief, thereby seeming to throw their weight behind what turns out to be a fabrication.

Reverend John Lothrop, the man behind the early house that is the oldest part of the Sturgis Library complex in Barnstable, is central to the West

Barnstable church's interpretation of history. There is some uncertainty as to some facts of his early life. His date and place of birth are not shown, but he was baptized on December 20, 1584, in the village of Etton in the East Riding of Yorkshire. Customarily, newborns were baptized on the first Sabbath after their birth. Some writers have him educated at Oxford's Christ Church College, but it seems clear he graduated with a bachelor's degree from Queen's College, Cambridge, in 1605. Four years later, he earned a master's at the same school. After, he took holy orders and became the minister at Egerton, Kent County. Within about five years, he renounced the orders and separated from the Church of England. Lothrop moved to London and eventually became involved with the Independent or Congregational Society in the Southwark neighborhood. This was perilous behavior.

The frightful and bloody struggle for religious freedom in England went back many years. The rigidity of the Roman church ruled until Henry VIII in 1534 declared himself the head of the English church. With this declaration, Protestantism became the state religion. After Henry died in 1547, his son Edward, only nine years of age, inherited the throne. Since he had not reached maturity, a regency council governed. And the state became more Protestant. Fatally ill at fifteen, Edward VI tried to prevent either sister Mary or Elizabeth from succeeding him. He managed to get Lady Jane Grey installed, but it took Mary only nine days to depose and replace her. A Catholic, Mary I restored Rome's influence. Bloody repression of Protestants followed. Beheadings and quartering became common forms of punishment. When Mary died in 1558, her half sister Elizabeth, a Protestant, ascended to the throne. She became head of the Church of England. Nonetheless, dissenters felt the system remained too formal. Elizabeth I died in 1603, followed on the throne by James I. He strictly enforced conformity at the outset but eased somewhat as time passed. When he died in 1625, Charles I took over. Shortly after, the new king went on to marry the Catholic Bourbon princess Henrietta Maria of France. Protestant reformists feared another shift back toward Rome and Popish practices.

Reformation, as it can be seen, dominated and disordered public affairs. To try to get a handle on things, King Charles I appointed William Laud archbishop of Canterbury in 1633, intent on forcing conformity and rule by bishops. Severe persecution of dissenters continued, including reliance on the notorious Star Chamber.

By this time, Britons found themselves in one of four religious categories. They were members of the Church of England, Roman Catholics, Puritans or Separatists. The Puritans objected to and opposed the formalities in practice. The Separatists, also known as Brownists, wanted a complete break from the rigidity of the state church. Named after the charismatic Robert Browne, who appeared in Norwich in 1580 espousing his breakaway views, his followers faced severe reprisals. The authorities jailed the rebellious Browne thirty-two times before exiling him to Holland. In an unexpected turn, after a time, Browne dropped his opposition and returned to the fold. "[H]e is by one side persistently described as the founder of Congregationalism....From having advocated Congregational principles at one part of his career, and withdrawn from them at another, he has received scant justice from both sides."[34] *Britannica* considers Browne the founder of Congregationalism.

The church historian Dale asserts: "The first regularly constituted English Congregational Church of which any record or tradition remains was the church of which Richard Fitz was pastor."[35] While meeting regularly every week, on June 19, 1567, Fitz retained Plumbers Hall in London for a weekly service, telling the hall-keeper he wanted it for a wedding. The sheriff knew otherwise and sent his men to arrest Fitz and a number of his followers. Some managed to escape over the rooftops and down the alleys. A lengthy and recorded trial followed. Fitz would die in prison. The Fitz story, it is said, provides "indisputable evidence of the existence of a Congregational Church in London as early as 1571, which must have been in existence there for some years, for its pastor, Richard Fitz, had already died in prison."[36]

At about this time, Sir Walter Raleigh declared in Parliament as many as twenty thousand people were gathered in several independent congregations in Essex, Norfolk and London. The congregation about London formed a church under Francis Johnson in 1592. The oldest son of the mayor of Richmond, North Riding of Yorkshire, he was born in 1562. Educated at Christ College, Cambridge, he would go on to write the primary Brownist document. In the summer, Johnson's congregation met early on the Sabbath in open fields. In the colder weather, they were forced to meet in private homes. After much trouble with the authorities, he fled to Holland. He died in exile in 1618 but had a great influence on the independent movement.

As well, there is Reverend John Robinson to consider. Known as the pastor of the Pilgrim Fathers, he was born in 1575 in Sturton-Le Steeple, Nottinghamshire. Educated at Corpus Christi College, he was ordained a priest of the Church of England in 1598. In less than a decade, he became involved with Separatists around Scrooby, and he left the church in 1606 after much hesitancy and reflection. Robinson spent many years in Leyden, where he died in March 1625. He expected to leave for New England in 1620, but the boat scheduled to accompany the *Mayflower* became unseaworthy, forcing Robinson and others to stay behind. Daniel Neal claims Robinson first started the Congregational or independent form of church. And John Brown adds that Robinson served as "pastor of the Congregational church in the city of Norwich."[37] He sets the date soon after 1600. In any event, it had to be before 1609, when Robinson fled to Leyden. Obviously, Robinson followed Browne and Fitz, but to the matter at hand, he preceded the 1616 Southwark church by about a decade.

Adding to the contention, for a good many years, the Pilgrim Fathers Church in Southwark claimed direct descent to the 1616 gathering. Its structure suffered severe damage during the bombings of World War II. Closed or merged about 2005, nonetheless, it was on the scene when the West Parish first set forth its case of originality.

Finally, it is known that separate religious gatherings took place in England as early as the 1380s in the time of the theologian and Oxford professor John Wycliffe. So, the West Parish claim of outright originality is questionable. But that is not the sole point. As much at issue is continuity. Can the West Barnstable church trace an uninterrupted chain back to the congregation that came together in Southwark in 1616? Scrutiny of the record provides an answer.

Henry Jacob starts things off. Born in 1563 in Cheriton, Kent, Jacob received his education at St. Mary Hall, Oxford, graduating with a master's degree in 1586. For a period, he served as a precentor at Oxford's Corpus Christi College. Before long, in 1590, he became a Brownist and followed a gathering in exile to Holland. He returned to England in 1597. After listening to the prominent Anglican bishop of Worcester hold forth on Christ's descent into hell as treated in the Apostle's Creed, he wrote a piece in opposition to the views expressed. Soon, he again felt the need to head across the channel to Holland. Known as a semi-separatist, he agreed the Church of England was the true church but felt it needed thorough reform. This moderate position placed him at odds with hardline Brownists such as Francis Johnson. Jacob and John Robinson, it should be noted, greatly influenced each other. In 1616, Jacob returned to London and formed the Southwark church at issue. Six years later, in 1622, he left the pastorate eventually to John Lothrop and headed for Virginia, where he died two years later.

John Lothrop led the congregation of some sixty members for eight years. Forced to meet in secret, on April 22, 1632, they surreptitiously gathered at the home of Humphrey Barnet in the Black Friars section of London. Laud learned of the clandestine meeting and sent his pursuivant Tomlinson to make arrests. His squad nabbed forty-two, while eighteen managed to

Henry Jacob Sunday poster. *Private collection.*

escape. After trials, the guilty went to the nearby Clink prison or to the Newgate facility. Lothrop may have served his time at both places.

While Lothrop was in prison, his wife, Hannah, became fatally ill. The authorities granted him the opportunity to visit her before she expired. When he returned to prison, he left his six children to struggle alone on the streets, begging for food and shelter. All of the other detainees by this time had gained their release. Lothrop, however, posed too much of a threat to be set loose. Moreover, he refused to take the oath ex officio. This abusive oath came into use at this period of religious turmoil as a form of intimidation, ill treatment and forced self-incrimination. Opposition to its practice eventually led to its abolishment and the establishment of the right not to incriminate oneself in the reforms that led up to the Habeas Corpus Act of 1649 and the end of the Star Chamber. In time, the situation with the Lothrop children at large prompted Bishop Laud to relent. Some believe Lothrop had made a direct personal appeal for leniency to King Charles. Be this as it may, in May 1634, the bishop set Lothrop free with the understanding that he would promptly get out of England and leave for the American colonies.

On August 1, 1634, Lothrop and his children boarded the three-hundred-ton *Griffin* and sailed out of the Downs to America. John Gallop brought the ship into Boston Harbor on September 18, seven weeks out. The one hundred passengers had company—some one hundred head of cattle. During this decade, stock farming was the most profitable business in New England. Of the passengers, thirty-two were former members of the Southwark church. And there was another person on board who would gain broad and lasting fame. Anne Hutchinson became a leading religious dissenter who confronted Puritan leadership. She insisted she had the right to hold religious services in her own dwelling as she saw fit. Eventually excommunicated and banished from the Massachusetts Bay Colony, she wound up on what is Aquidneck Island, Rhode Island. A member of the National Women's Hall of Fame, she is viewed as an early feminist.

Lothrop remained in Boston for just a short period, but long enough for Governor John Winthrop of the Province of Massachusetts Bay to make a telling observation in his journal, to wit:

> *Mr. Lathrop…being at Boston upon a sacrament day, after the sermon, etc. desired leave of the congregation to be present at the administration, etc., but said that he durst not desire to partake in it, because he was not then in order, (being dismissed from his former congregation,) and he thought it not fit to be suddenly admitted into any other, for example sake, and because of the deceitfulness of man's heart. He went to Scituate, being desired to be their pastor.*[38]

This contemporary observation admits of but one meaning. Lothrop did not travel to the colonies with the Southwark church on his back. By his own words, Lothrop had been discharged from the London church. Preeminent Cape Cod historian Charles F. Swift felt the Winthrop observation leads to one conclusion: "The claim that the West Barnstable church represents the first Independent church organization can hardly be sustained."[39]

Amos Otis reached the same conclusion by expanding the argument. Passengers departing England for America at the time were required to obtain a certificate from the administrator or minister of their town or village attesting to their good character and conformity with the Church of England. And they had to take an oath of allegiance. To be able to take the oath, Lothrop would have been required to renounce his orders as a pastor. His statement to Winthrop supports the view that Lothrop took such a step. Out of this, Otis concludes, "The above facts prove conclusively that the Barnstable church is an offshoot of the London, not the church itself."[40] Reverend Hiram Carleton, an early and committed proponent of the West Barnstable church's claim, took great exception to the Otis position. Carleton served as the West Parish minister from 1853 to 1862. "I cannot concede," he declared. "I see no good reason for denying to the West Barnstable church the right to regard its tradition as founded in *probable* [emphasis added] facts of history."[41]

Winthrop's observation, it is fair, must be viewed alongside Reverend Cotton Mather's discussion of early New England pastors, a generalized view that can be interpreted to conflict with the governor. Mather places Lothrop in the First Class of seventy-seven early ministers or those who

The 1717 Meetinghouse tower topped by the 1723 gilded rooster weathervane. *J.H. Ellis.*

"were in the *actual exercise* of their ministry when they left *England* and were the instruments of bringing the *gospel* into the wilderness, and of settling churches here according to the order of the *gospel*."[42] Mather does not treat the oath of allegiance matter as it may have affected some of the departing ministers. Any who took the oath, as did Lothrop, would not have been "in the *actual exercise* of their ministry" when they boarded their boat to America. Moreover, Mather says the men brought the gospel with them, not their churches. Charles Chauncey, Joseph Hull and John Mayo, who appear below, also are included in the ambiguous First Class list.

Shortly after the Winthrop interview, Lothrop headed for nearby Scituate to the south and became the town's first regularly settled minister. With a fine harbor fronting Massachusetts Bay, the area attracted Plymouth families as early as 1627. Incorporation followed in 1636. Previously, on January 18, 1634, OS (Old Style), a church gathered and selected Lothrop as its guide. "The ceremonies of induction into office were the laying on of the hands of the elders with prayers."[43] Lothrop took up residence on a twenty-acre farm on the southeast side of Coleman hills near the first herring brook. He also held shares in the New Harbor marshes between the North River and his house.

"His ministry here was not prosecuted with great success or in much peace." In February 1638, he wrote to Plymouth governor Thomas Prince, advising, "Many grievances attend me." He beseeched Prince for "a place for the transplanting of us." And he requested the governor intercede with "the Indians for the place…and we will freely give satisfaction to them."[44] At first, Scituate families had their eyes on Sippican or Rochester on the South Coast along Buzzards Bay. But by the next year, the Great Marshes of Barnstable appeared much more attractive. The salt marshes promised inexhaustive amounts of hay and thatch. Cattle seemed to prefer the various saltwater grasses. And there appeared to be unlimited room for livestock and crops in Barnstable.

In his correspondence with the Plymouth governor, it is noteworthy that Lothrop diplomatically described his grievances in general terms. There were problems associated with the meetinghouse. Scituate historian Samuel Deane felt the matter of baptism was at the center of the strife. But Otis convincingly says that was not the case. For some years, the English Independent churches had been embroiled in a major controversy on the topic. The dispute centered on whether sprinkling was sufficient or if immersion was necessary. Frederick Freeman may have been more on point. He believes the "discontent" involved insufficient land. Lothrop, Timothy Hatherly and Goodman Annable had appealed to the General Court, saying "that they had but small portions of land in Scituate, and, notwithstanding lands were subsequently set off to them between North and South rivers, difficulties of an embarrassing nature were thought to attend the location."[45]

Abiel Holmes, after mentioning the "broken condition" of the Scituate church, indicates, "The Rev. John Lothrop, with *part* [emphasis added] of that church, removed to Cape Cod."[46] Be this as it may, advance Scituate transplants showed up in Barnstable (previously known as Mattakeesett) in late June 1639 ahead of two main contingents. Lothrop and a band followed by land, arriving on October 10, 1639, OS. Deacon Henry Cobb led the second group and came in by way of the water the next day. The primary moves were delayed until autumn so as to enable the gathering of their annual Scituate crops. Incorporated as the Town of Barnstable on June 14, 1639, the place took its name from Barnstaple, Devonshire, an English port from which many of the emigrants departed to America.

Two ministers, Reverend Joseph Hull and Reverend John Mayo, already resided in town, but there is not a record of an organized church. And of course, a meetinghouse did not exist. Upon arrival of the newcomers, Hull opened his house for a thanksgiving service recognizing their safe and healthy move. Obviously, however, Barnstable did not need three ministers. Mayo turned out to be the easiest to deal with. In 1640, the Lothrop church made him a teaching elder. Six years later, he moved to Nauset to head the church in what became the town of Eastham. A decade later, Mayo transferred to a Boston pastorate.

Hull, however, proved difficult. Governor Winthrop considered him contentious. Hull had ministered in Weymouth beforehand and devoted much of his time to cattle trading. Considered just about the most important man in Barnstable before Lothrop's arrival, he also served in leading civil positions. In 1641, he moved to neighboring Yarmouth to lead a band of discontented people from both towns. Barnstable excommunicated him as a consequence. Since he stepped on the toes of the settled Yarmouth minister, Reverend Marmaduke Mathews, the General Court threatened to arrest him. Hull drifted back to Barnstable, acknowledged his sins and gained back acceptance in Lothrop's church. Soon, he moved to Dover, New Hampshire, to head that town's church. And Lothrop became the uncontested religious leader in Barnstable.

At the outset under Lothrop, when weather permitted, religious meetings were held outside. Otherwise, a relatively large dwelling could accommodate a limited audience. Tradition indicates a huge boulder served as a favorite backdrop for outdoor services, suggestive of Peter "and upon this rock I will build My church." Hull, it is said, started the practice. A large glacial erratic fitting the description was cut down the middle in 1820 and half used for the foundation of the first local jail. Years later, the town broke up the remaining half and used the rubble as road fill. More recently, some of the remnant pieces were recovered from the road and formed into a Sacrament Rock monument alongside the present Old Kings Highway.

As we have seen, Lothrop built his second house in 1644, and it was large enough to accommodate a modest number of church members for religious services. His first primitive house was located in what is now the commercial or business district in the center of the village. The first meetinghouse went up two years later, just west of what became the burying ground. Lothrop died on November 8, 1653. Ten years would pass before the church could agree on a replacement, although Reverend William Sargeant led services for a time right after Lothrop. Reverend Thomas Walley served from 1663 until his death in 1678. This time it took only five contentious years to agree on a new minister. Reverend Jonathan Russell served from 1683 until his passing in 1711. Prior to his arrival, the parish replaced its meetinghouse with a new building in 1681. The senior Russell was succeeded in a year by his son Jonathan Russell II.

In 1715, the town voted to authorize two meetinghouses. It is important to note that the early meetinghouses of New England were municipal buildings used for town meetings and the like as well as religious services. Two years later, Barnstable voted to set off two precincts, cutting the town in half. The division did not go smoothly. A year earlier, two dozen men, without approval, had started to build a new meetinghouse in what would become the East Parish. Reverend Russell protested the premature construction, and it became necessary to seat an Ecclesiastical Council to resolve the dispute. The council found each side had displayed "too much heat" and recommended the church accept the facts on the ground and "make no further animadversions."[47]

When it came time for Russell to make a choice between the East and West Parishes, few had any doubt about the direction he would take. He, of course, moved to the West Parish and their new meetinghouse and, perhaps, a more supportive congregation. His first service in West Barnstable took place on Thanksgiving Day 1719. Russell carried along all the church records, communion silver and pewter sacramental vessels. The East objected and wanted a fair share of the valuable silver. In order to avoid another Ecclesiastical Council, the West relented and sent back two of the four silver communion vessels. This closed the matter.

Thus, the split was completed. More to the point made by backers of the "original church" legend, the move represented the final step in the Southwark/Scituate/Barnstable/West Barnstable journey.

There are two components to the legend. First, it is said Lothrop came to America conveying the Southwark church. We have seen that did not happen. Second, if that had been the case, the Southwark church ceased to exist upon his departure. Henry C. Kittredge, the third distinguished Cape Cod historian to disbelieve the legend, did so because the Southwark church continued "after Lothrop's departure from it."[48] The Southwark church not only continued in place but went on to make a broader name for itself in religious circles. Considered the leading or mother church of the movement called Particular Baptist, it is known as the J-L-J or Jacob-Lothrop-Jessey church. Reverend Henry Jessey replaced Lothrop at Southwark in 1637 and, as indicated by the third letter in the abbreviated designation, carried on the work of the church.

Born in 1601 in West Rowton near Northallerton, Yorkshire, Jessey was a minister's son. Upon graduation in 1624 from St. John's College, Cambridge, he went on to become a noted Hebrew scholar. For a time, he tutored for a family at Arington, Suffolk. In 1633, he became a vicar in Aughton, Yorkshire. Jessey continued to move about, and as indicated, in 1637, he took over the Southwark church. For years, the church repeatedly faced opposition and often changed its meeting place to avoid detection. The bishop's enforcers carried away the entire congregation in February 1638. Harassment continued, so the large congregation decided to split up. Half went with Praise-God Barebone, a leather-seller and former elder in a Leyden Separatist church. He had an older brother named Fear-God, and his father served as the rector in Charwelton, Northamptonshire. Arrests remained common. Jessey briefly traveled to Holland to obtain the independent rights of some former followers. Shortly after returning to England, he fell ill and died in September 1663, bringing an end to the J-L-J era.

The path of the church after its split is difficult to trace. As for Barebone, by late 1641, he was preaching to large audiences at his own place, as many as 150 people at a time. Later, he became a member of the extreme Puritan sect known as Fifth Monarchists. In the final analysis, tracing the history of the church after Jessey is unnecessary to make the argument against the West Parish claim of originality. All that is required is to show the Southwark church continued after Lothrop left the country. Recounting Jessey's tenure, however brief, makes the case.

In summary, the West Parish church claims it is the very same church that gathered in Southwark, London, England, in 1616, its direct, unbroken descent the result of Reverend John Lothrop's move to New England carrying the church with him. But the assertion fails when it is recalled, notwithstanding Cotton Mather, that Governor John Winthrop recorded Lothrop's admission that he came as a private individual, not as a minister with his congregation. True, some of his London congregation were on the same boat from England and joined him in Scituate and followed him to Barnstable. But they did not leave their homeland as an organized church. They traveled as a plain gathering of individuals. Further, a review of Jessey's tenure at the Southwark church demonstrates the church, although it was changing its direction, continued after Lothrop's departure from England. The church did not relocate to America. Emphasis must be placed on the *J* that follows the *L* in the often-used J-L-J contraction. This demonstrates someone followed Lothrop at the church he left in London. And the fact that three eminent Cape Cod historians—Henry C. Kittredge, Amos Otis and Charles F. Swift—reject the West Parish view of history is compelling. Moreover, a fourth highly respected Cape Cod historian, Frederick Freeman, hesitates to accept the chain of events underlying the West Parish claim. In discussing the step to Barnstable in 1639, he notes, "It has sometimes been said that 'the Scituate church' came; it is, doubtless, proper to state that a *majority* of the male members of that church came."[49] He adds, quoting Holmes in *American Annals*: "The residue immediately reorganized and called Rev. Chas. Chauncey to become their pastor."[50] Chauncey took over in 1641. (He would go on to become president of Harvard.) This certainly puts a different spin on things. That supposedly authoritative sources such as the Congregational Library & Archives, the National Register of Historic Places and numerous writers repeat the false claim is immaterial. They simply repeat what is offered without vetting the information. Cross-checking can be tedious work.

When the accuracy of a cherished piece of historical lore is challenged if not debunked, adherents react in various ways. Some fret and resist. Others readily and good-naturedly accept the facts and move on. Figures from the distant past, however, are especially vulnerable to inaccurate biographical material. Damaging information is the most harmful since seldom is someone living with a motivated interest to dig deep and correct the record. On the other hand, there are occasions when exaggerated accomplishments are credited to a historic figure. Too often, overstatement is accepted without question. The recent interest in a formerly overlooked feminist will demonstrate.

CHAPTER 4

FAMOUS ATTRACT UNTRUTH

Mercy Otis Warren, born in West Barnstable in 1728, may well be the most important woman ever born on Cape Cod. Granted, even a qualified absolute statement like the foregoing is open to doubt. Nonetheless, supporting evidence is compelling. Mercy is the only Cape woman to be an inductee in the National Women's Hall of Fame in Seneca Falls, New York. Much too much time passed before she received this high honor in 2002. Warren did not begin to be fully appreciated until the latter part of the twentieth century. A cursory search suggests more biographical books have been written about her than any other Cape native, many of them in recent years. The belated enthusiasm may have prompted the exaggerated claims some admirers attach to the woman.

Warren has been described "as the 'invisible' author of the Bill of Rights."[51] In another instance, she is called "the woman who inspired the Bill of Rights."[52] More generally, she is depicted as "the champion of the nation's Bill of Rights."[53] As a result of this kind of overstatement, there are people who simply believe she actually wrote the first ten amendments to the Constitution. In a sense, her role in the matter proved noteworthy, but it did not rise to such a decisive level. By contrast, Alice Brown's fairly detailed 1890 biography of Mercy does not even mention the Constitution or the controversy that swirled about the Bill of Rights question. The same can be said for Mary Beth Norton's *Liberty's Daughters* and other early books.

By birth and marriage, Mercy was destined to be close to the great events of her time. Her father, James Otis Sr., served as a militia colonel; speaker of

A photograph of the painting of Mercy Otis Warren by John Singleton Copley. *Courtesy of the W.B. Nickerson Archives, Cape Cod Community College.*

the House of Representatives; judge of probate; chief justice of the Court of Common Pleas; member of the Governor's Council; and since he was the senior member of that body when British general Thomas Gage vacated Boston and the governor's role, the elder Otis became chief executive magistrate of the province until the adoption of the state constitution, a period of five years.

Mercy's older brother James Otis Jr., known as the Patriot to history and Jemmy to the family, was the intellectual leader of the anti-British movement in prewar Massachusetts and a prominent and connected Boston lawyer.

Another brother, Samuel, served as clerk of the U.S. Senate during its first twenty-five years. Although he had a fine career, he is best known for holding the Bible for Washington as the general was inaugurated as the first president. He served as speaker of the Massachusetts House of Representatives and as a delegate to the Second Continental Congress. And General Joseph Otis, a third brother, as well as a ranking militia officer, served in the legislature; was clerk of the Court of Common Pleas; and was collector of customs in Barnstable.

When Mercy married James Warren of Plymouth in 1754, she paired two distinguished old-line families. Warren, the son of a wealthy merchant, went on to serve as president of the third Massachusetts Provincial Congress; speaker of the Massachusetts House of Representatives; major general in the Massachusetts militia; and paymaster general of the Continental army.

These links exposed Mercy to leading participants in the resistance to Great Britain, such as Samuel Adams and the notorious Dr. Benjamin Church. As well, she had close contact with politicians, including Elbridge Gerry and John Hancock. Mercy also became familiar with military leaders from Alexander Hamilton up to General George Washington. And she had a lengthy and intimate friendship with John and Abigail Adams. "Between John and Mercy, there was…a special relationship. Both quick-witted, they bantered back and forth, teased, made bargains and when they were all together in the Warrens' parlor, they 'drew characters,' as they called it; they described and did takeoffs on people they knew. But perhaps more satisfying for two people who thrived on praise, they loved to compliment each other."[54]

In addition to connections, for a girl of her era, Mercy received a fair education. Colonel Otis enlisted the most educated man in the village, Yale graduate Reverend Jonathan Russell II, to tutor two sons, Jemmy and Joseph. Russell had married into the extended Otis family. Jemmy sensed curious Mercy felt left out. In the evenings, he shared his lessons and books with her. In time, it became obvious Joseph was a mediocre student. The colonel, a self-taught man who valued learning, made a switch. Joseph went to work in the family store, and Mercy took his place in Russell's parlor. "James Otis wanted every advantage for his children. How could he say no to a formal education for any of them, even a girl?"[55]

As Reverend Russell continued through the next few years to prepare Jemmy for college, Mercy maintained her fervor for learning. She showed a passion for history, and this prompted the minister to loan her a copy of Sir Walter Raleigh's *History of the World*. Mercy remained isolated in West Barnstable when her brother went off to Harvard. His commencement in 1743 may have been a turning point in her life. When she traveled to Cambridge for the event, she met James Warren, one of her brother's close friends at school. Some biographers figure this was her introduction to her future husband. Perhaps, but Colonel Otis and the senior Warren had been doing business with each other since the early 1730s. So, the couple may have met before the Harvard gathering. Be this as it may, once married, the pair settled in Plymouth proper. In a few years, James inherited the family estate along the Eel River outside of town. In the pastoral setting, Mercy found time to engage in her joy of writing.

The political events of the 1760s intensified Mercy's interest in public affairs. In February 1761, brother James Otis gained immortal fame with his four-hour fiery argument at trial on the evils of writs of assistance or general search warrants employed by British customs officials in Boston. From this point onward, the political climate in Massachusetts became heated and then hostile. Parliament in London passed one act after another, aimed at squeezing taxes and duties out of the colonists and gaining their obedience. Mercy noted these decrees spread "a general alarm throughout the continent."[56] Her brother James led the initial public challenge. In the space of just over a year, he authored four hugely persuasive pamphlets probing the broad question of taxation without representation. Some years later, Mercy recalled James as "the first American who with masterly precision investigated the rights and defended the liberties of his country."[57]

In 1768, Samuel Adams joined James Otis in making the now familiar taxation argument in what became known as the "Circular Letter" since it was distributed throughout the colonies. British authorities objected and demanded a retraction when the Massachusetts legislature adopted the letter. The General Court refused by a 92 to 17 vote. Infuriated, Great Britain ordered all colonial royal governors terminate their legislatures so the assemblies could not consider the disloyal document. In Plymouth, increasingly, the Warren home became a meeting place for those who shared the view of the letter. And Mercy began writing nonpolitical poems.

In the early 1770s, as her brother James slipped deeper into mental instability, another influential person crossed into Mercy's path, a role model so to speak. Catherine Macaulay, a famous British Whig writer and historian, communicated with colonial dissidents who shared her political philosophy, James Otis included. As Otis faded from the scene, Mercy began to fill the void. In June 1773, she wrote to Macaulay for the first time "though conscious inferiority checks the ambitious hope of a long correspondence." The correspondence would last until Macaulay's death in 1791. Mercy continued, "I thank you for the marks of esteem you have heretofore shown to a brother of mine, a Gentleman, eminent for his remarkable exertion of ability in behalf of the expiring liberties of his country." She hoped Macaulay could "honour these distant regions with a visit."[58] In 1784, Macaulay made such a trip, visiting Mount Vernon and the Washingtons as well as Plymouth and the Warrens.

In March 1770, the notorious Boston Massacre inflamed the province. The political climate in the town spiraled downward. Loyalists, or those who supported British rule, became objects of abuse. Nobody appeared more polarizing than Lieutenant Governor Thomas Hutchinson, who became governor in March 1771. Long at odds with the Otis family, he became a target for Mercy's pen. She wrote three political plays taking aim at the governor. Her first published work, "The Adulateur," appeared in the *Massachusetts Spy* newspaper in the spring of 1772, followed by "The Defeat" printed in the *Boston Gazette* in 1773 and "The Group," which came out in 1775. Published anonymously, the satirical plays promoted active resistance to royal authority.

John Adams was close enough to the Warrens to know Mercy's role in this business. When the famous December 1773 Boston Tea Party inflamed matters, he wrote to James Warren outlining a poem eulogizing the event. "I wish to see a late glorious event celebrated by a certain political pen which has no equal that I know of in this country."[59] Mercy accepted the challenge and wrote what can be described as her most important poem. In early 1774, "The Squabble of the Sea Nymphs" presented a mythical debate between Neptune's rival wives, Amphytrite and Salacia. Mercy crafted the poem to emphasize the influence of women contrasted to men in the recently adopted boycott of British tea. Adams expressed delight.

Mercy continued to write poems, some personal and others for publication. Jumping ahead to 1790, she wrote two additional plays, *The Sack of Rome* and *The Ladies of Castile*. *The Blockheads* in 1776, *The Motley Assembly* in 1779 and *Sans Souci* in 1785 may have come from her pen, but authorship is unproven. Her most important writing remained in the future.

As is well known, armed conflict and open rebellion started in Lexington in April 1775. Mercy became a war widow while James went off to service. He sat on the Navy Board for six years and acted as paymaster for the army for a year. While a major general in the militia, he was tapped to lead a campaign in Rhode Island but declined and resigned over an issue involving his authority. Meanwhile, in fits and starts, Mercy began work on her magnum opus: the *History of the Rise, Progress and Termination of the American Revolution Interspersed with Biographical, Political and Moral Observations.* The three-volume work of 1,298 pages would not appear until 1805. This proved unique work for a woman, especially since she wrote from a female perspective. Mercy utilized all available sources, including personal memory, corresponding and conversing with participants, public records, state papers, letters and published material. And she took the then unusual step of footnoting sources.

Long before her history appeared, Mercy wrote the piece that now defines her to so many. Developments over time thrust her and James Warren into the middle of the Massachusetts debate over a new national constitution.

In September 1774, responding to Great Britain's repressive acts, delegates from twelve of the thirteen colonies met in Philadelphia as the First Continental Congress. Georgia did not attend since it had its hands full with hostile Indigenous tribes and it needed the help of British troops. A year later, with war underway, the colonies met again as the Second Continental Congress. And of course, on July 4, 1776, the colonies declared independence. In another year, Congress adopted the initial constitutional document—the Articles of Confederation. Ratification did not follow until 1781. But it did not take long to demonstrate the document's deficiencies.

The Articles created a league of equal member states but without the dependable ability to raise operating funds. States did not always see the need to pay assessed U.S. taxes. A state or two declined to pay any of their assessments. This meant the country was unable to defend itself as a unified force. Some states even unilaterally negotiated with foreign powers. Congress needed nine states to agree to proposed measures, and sometimes all thirteen had to assent.

A notorious series of incidents beginning in 1786 in western Massachusetts highlighted the weakness of the system of decentralized government. Shays' Rebellion was a string of fierce attacks on courthouses and other public property by financially stressed farmers objecting to high taxes, lack of credit and foreclosures.

Reacting, in early 1787, Congress called for a convention to revise the Articles in order to address obvious shortcomings. Nationalists pointed to the rebellion as a reason for a new constitution that would provide for a strong federal or centralized government while reducing states' rights. Henry

Knox, a notable wartime general, wrote to George Washington reporting on the Shays' affair and urging him to attend the convention. "[S]omething is wanting and something must be done or we shall be involved in all the horror of faction and civil war."[60]

The convention gathered in Philadelphia in May 1787 with the broad charge "to revise the Articles of Confederation to render the Federal Constitution adequate to the exigencies of government and the preservation of the Union."[61] Nationalists, or those in favor of a strong central government, prevailed from the outset, although the other side pushed its states' rights and individual liberty philosophies. Delegate Elbridge Gerry of Massachusetts, a Warren ally, became a continuing critic of the nationalistic or federal positions. Luther Martin, a Maryland delegate, joined in the criticism. In the end, the nationalists, otherwise known as Federalists, prevailed and approved a completely new constitution. Gerry declined to sign the finished document, and Martin left before the convention ended. Gerry felt compelled to explain his Anti-Federalist position in a letter to the Massachusetts General Court. He claimed in the final product "that some of the powers of the [national] legislature are ambiguous, and others indefinite and dangerous...and that the system is without the security of a bill of rights."[62]

In the fall of 1787, the proposed constitution went to the states for ratification. James Warren promptly wrote six well-crafted essays advocating rejection of the document, mirroring Gerry's concerns. His work appeared in the *Massachusetts Centinel* under the pen names Helvidius Priscus and A Republican Federalist. Fellow Anti-Federalist James Winthrop of Boston joined Warren, writing under the pseudonym Agrippa. Not to be outdone, proponents put together a classic series of essays and contributed them to New York newspapers with a specific goal of influencing the ratification vote in that state. Authored by Alexander Hamilton, James Madison and John Jay, the pieces were collected in a book entitled *The Federalist.* The book remains influential to this day, especially when the intent of the founders is at issue.

At this point, it should be noted, the use of pen names with an underlying patriotic connotation was a common practice. Priscus was a stoic philosopher in early Rome, while Agrippa was a Roman statesman and general of the same period. *The Federalist* carried the signature of Publius, honoring the founder of the Roman Republic. Thus, when Mercy used pseudonyms, it did not seem out of order and just a means to disguise her gender. However, the problem with such a practice is we may never know the identity of some of these early commentators.

Mercy jumped into the fray in February 1788, writing a nineteen-page essay titled "Observations on the New Constitution, and on the Federal and State Conventions," signed by A Columbian Patriot. At the time, it was assumed Gerry authored the piece. Mercy's authorship was not settled until 1930. "Written in her typically bombastic, convoluted style," Mercy's work covered the same general points appearing in other critiques.[63] She complained of the absence of a bill of rights; the threat of a standing army; and the inadequacy of the proposed congress and system of representation. In brief, she saw "too much room for human error."[64] Like other critics, Mercy felt the proposed constitution would substitute one form of tyranny for the one the country had just cast out.

With this particular writing in mind, some current admirers exaggerate and give Mercy a great deal more credit than deserved when it comes to the creation of the Bill of Rights. In fact, at the time, Mercy's marginal role and importance in the debate were overshadowed by the opposing positions of a number of outspoken national luminaries. This group included Patrick Henry and his fellow Virginians Arthur Lee, George Mason and Edmund Randolph; Samuel Chase of Maryland; George Clinton and Robert Yates from New York; Rawlins Lowndes of South Carolina; and the aforementioned Gerry and Martin. To a lesser extent, Samuel Adams and John Hancock offered objections. As well, newspapers throughout the country took sides.

Ratification required acceptance by nine states. The process got underway quickly. Delaware led the way, approving the proposal in early December 1787. Pennsylvania, New Jersey, Georgia and Connecticut followed, approving by the beginning of the second week in 1788. Just as Mercy's "Observations" was to appear in February, led by Samuel Adams and John Hancock, the Anti-Federalists negotiated a remedial bargain to break the deadlock that had developed in Boston. Known as the Massachusetts Compromise, under its terms, the Anti-Federalists in the legislature agreed to vote for the constitution as submitted since the Federalists in turn agreed to support amendments creating a bill of rights. The Commonwealth ratified on February 6. Five other states took the Massachusetts approach. When New Hampshire accepted on June 23, the new constitution took effect. The four remaining sates followed. Rhode Island, the last state, accepted in May 1790. By this time, the new form of government had been in place for more than a year.

The Massachusetts Compromise cleared the way for amendments to follow ratification rather than precede approval. Many of the key participants feared a second constitutional convention since it could open the door to undoing what had been accomplished. Also, some felt another convention so soon after the first would tend to shake public confidence in the system. Therefore, amendments would be addressed by the congressional process. James Madison, who now thought amendments useful but not necessary, received the assignment to draft the amendments the Anti-Federalists were seeking. He drew heavily on the Magna Carta, the English Bill of Rights, history in general and the 1776 Virginia Declaration of Rights. Anti-Federalist George Mason's influence once again came to the forefront since he drafted much of the Virginia document, which declared all men had certain inherent rights.

As a member of the House of Representatives in the First Congress, Madison's goal was to shift thinking from what the government could do to declaring what it could not do. Individual rights and limitations on federal and state governments were to be guaranteed. He prepared nine amendments to this end, but the full House went on to add eight and approve seventeen. The Senate then pared the number down to twelve.

In September 1789, the dozen amendments went to the states for their approval. Three-fourths of the states had to favor the amendments before they could take effect. The process wound up taking over two years, with final adoption of amendment numbers three through twelve on December 15, 1791. The ten endorsed amendments became known as the Bill of Rights.

In the end, Mercy's part in the entire process proved to be imperceptible. She turned out to be just one of a great many "champions" of the Bill of Rights and by no means its "invisible" author. Her distinction is she appeared to be the only woman involved in the process even if in a limited and anonymous way. Interestingly, her brother James Otis Jr., dead for almost a decade, had his fingerprints all over the final document. The Fourth Amendment prohibiting unreasonable searches and seizures drew heavily on his earlier efforts against the British writs of assistance.

Undeserved adulation for someone like Mercy Otis Warren can be accepted and to a certain extent is understandable. But an untrue statement that besmirches one's reputation is intolerable. A legendary Cape Cod seaman suffered such an undeserved fate. Captain John "Mad Jack" Percival, born in West Barnstable in 1779, fell victim to insufficient research and poor analysis on the part of a distinguished biographer. The late Donald F. Long, University of New Hampshire professor emeritus of history, wrote a 1991 Percival biography that included a false and damaging judgment of the captain's character. Long reviewed Percival's handling of a trust in the

Captain John Percival (1779–1862), by Chester Harding. *U.S. Navy Department.*

supposed amount of $12,862 set up for six sailors injured in an 1836 railroad accident and reached a wholly erroneous "inescapable conclusion" that Percival "robbed unlettered and impoverished seamen of their little recompense" and made off with the entire amount.[65]

A problem with a falsehood of this nature is it endures. Later writers consult Long's work and repeat what they find. As one example, a respected Cape Cod author, referencing Long, covered the incident in his discussion of Percival and wrote, "'Mad Jack' became trustee and, to simplify a very long, tortuous story, he never paid them [injured sailors] any of their compensation. The amount is listed in his estate at death. He stole the compensation."[66]

The tale begins on June 29, 1836, when an eleven-car Boston and Providence Rail Road passenger train traveling northward on a single track smashed head-on into a three-car southbound train on the same track in Roxbury, Massachusetts. One railroad hand was killed and a number of passengers were injured, including sailors transferring from the Brooklyn yard to the Boston yard. The train line offered overnight travel between New York and Boston by joining with a water service. Boats ran between New York and Providence, connecting with train service between Rhode Island and Boston.

The single-track system carried a built-in risk. Poor weather could delay the New York boat's arrival by up to twelve hours. Thus, the train out of Providence had an irregular schedule. Regularly scheduled trains traveling in either direction followed a simple safety protocol. The first train to reach the midpoint in Foxboro pulled into a siding, thereby giving the opposing train clear and safe passage. The flawed system caught up with the rail company on a Wednesday late in June 1836.

A total of 300 passengers left New York the previous evening on the side-wheel steamer *Benjamin Franklin*. The total included 120 sailors and marines who made their way onto the cars in Providence. They were headed for new assignments on board the sloop-of-war *Boston*, 18 (i.e., rated for eighteen guns), waiting in the stream in Boston Harbor. The "steamboat train" left Providence at 10:00 a.m. and rushed into the longest straight stretch of track in the region, a 16.1-mile-long air line. Almost 38 miles out, the engineer slowed down approaching a siding near Forest Hills. Both he and the conductor knew a local train was scheduled to head south out of Boston at 12:30 p.m. The conductor checked his watch, pondered and then ordered the engineer to dash ahead. As it turned out, the conductor's watch was five minutes slow. Nearing a final siding in Roxbury, the anxious engineer slowed and turned to the conductor. He received another go-ahead command. He put on all steam and roared into Roxbury at 20 miles per hour, whipped through a high cut and around a bend. A startled flagman stationed at the hazardous curve frantically waved his flag, warning of a train approaching from the other direction. But it was too late.

The resulting collision was horrendous. Driven back, the engine of the "steamboat train" crushed its two leading cars. Passengers flew about. Some twenty servicemen received injuries. As soon as the dust settled, in an attempt to get ahead of things, the train company fired the conductor. Almost as soon, some of the injured sailors brought suit against the company. Coincidentally, Chief Justice Lemuel Shaw of the Massachusetts Supreme Judicial Court, a boyhood friend of Percival's, heard the case. In a memorable charge to the jury, Shaw said: "The law does not require precaution against all possible danger, but a reasonable and proper precaution, adapted to the nature of the case."[67] The jury determined the company did not meet the reasonable and proper test and awarded a total of $8,359 divided among six injured sailors. Long incorrectly indicated the award totaled $12,862.

Percival had just assumed duty as the executive officer at the Boston Navy Yard. He agreed to act as trustee in the case because, as he told an acquaintance, the six men were "penniless sailors, maimed and crippled without friends." Beforehand, he made sure he was "fully and clearly exempted from all trustee and other vexatious suits by artful and designing landlords and landladies."[68]

A brief review of Percival's career shows it was natural for him to volunteer as a trustee in such a case and faithfully carry out the task. More important, any objective scrutiny of the man will indicate larceny was not in his makeup. His character was well defined.

In the age of sail, Percival became the only man from Cape Cod to rise to the top in the U.S. Navy. Above all, those who knew him considered him a superior seaman. On a cruise to the Mediterranean in the second-class ship sloop *Cyane*, 22, Midshipman Henry A. Wise maintained a journal. Although often at odds with his captain, Wise recorded, "There is not a better sailor in the world than Cap. Percival or a man of better judgement in the qualities requisite for a Seaman....I would rather trust my life to his charge in case of emergency at Sea than any other man in the United States Navy."[69]

While off Madagascar in the *Constitution*, 44, in 1843, another midshipman wrote, "My only wish is that more commanders felt the way our Captain Percival felt towards the proper handling of a ship. To watch him is to watch a fine surgeon at work, and he takes his work as seriously as a physician as well."[70] His fellow officers thought as much. Esteemed Commodore Isaac Hull simply declared Percival "the best sailor I ever saw."[71]

Compassion for his crews also defined Percival. There were numerous times he made his cabin available to sick crew members. In one instance, on the *Cyane* cruise, seaman Nathaniel Sidney fell fatally ill with tuberculosis. He spent his final days in Percival's cabin. On a Pacific mission in the *Dolphin*, 12, "Mad Jack" sustained a double hernia while clearing the main boom. No more than a month later, he went ashore on an uninhabited islet with six sailors. A storm suddenly arose, and when the party tried to return to the ship, thunderous breakers smashed their boat. Five men swam to the *Dolphin* while Percival helped a nonswimmer back to shore. His lieutenant rigged a breeches buoy and got the stranded pair back to the ship. The crew took note of their disabled skipper's concern for one of his men.

While in the Caribbean with the *Porpoise*, 12, he again demonstrated his interest in the welfare of his crews. He went to the aid of the Bath, Maine merchantman *Java*, wrecked on the coast of Cuba. Captain Nathaniel Jefferson was so happy with the navy's help in saving most of his cargo that he sent a $600 reward to the *Porpoise*. Percival directed the entire reward go to his sailors, exclusive of officers.

As one of his last acts, in his will, Percival left $1,000 to the Massachusetts General Hospital to "be invested as a permanent fund, and the interest and income thereof to be appropriated for a free bed or free beds—and, as this is the gift of a poor old sailor, preference shall always be given to mariners."[72]

Percival is viewed as colorful. He served in four wars and in three navies, two as an impressed seaman. In between, he chased pirates in the Caribbean. Adding to the legend, his first and last ships are national shrines. The HMS *Victory*, 104, is dry-docked in Portsmouth, England, and the USS *Constitution* is berthed in Boston.

This background fascinated well-known writers. James Michener based a character in *Hawaii* on "Mad Jack." Herman Melville, personally acquainted with Percival, modeled a key character in *White Jacket* after his friend. In the novel, Melville describes the fictional Lieutenant Mad Jack as "a bit of a tyrant—they say all good officers are—but the sailors loved him all round;

and would much rather stand fifty watches with him, than one with a rose-water sailor."[73] By all accounts, this is a fair depiction of the real man.

Nathaniel Hawthorne, the first novelist to write about Percival, visited the Boston Navy Yard with Maine congressman Jonathan Cilley in June 1837. During the course of the visit, they sat down with Percival, and Hawthorne took notes. The conversation turned to politics, and Percival took "the opposite side to Cilley, and arguing with much pertinacity. He seems to have molded and shaped himself to his own whims, till a sort of rough affectation has become thoroughly imbued throughout a kindly nature." In the end, Hawthorne concluded, "Percival seems to be the very pattern of old integrity."[74]

The foregoing does not suggest a dishonest person. But what do the trust records show?

Percival maintained a detailed accounting of his handling of the funds entrusted to him. The award provided $3,000 to Joshua Howell; $2,250 each to Thomas Murdock and James Thompson; $1,500 to Charles White; and $175 each to John Cummings and Benjamin Ramson. Trust records are the major component of the John Percival Papers held by the Massachusetts Historical Society. Every single document generated by the trust is not found in the collection, but the relatively few missing are unimportant. A solid audit trail exists. And every Long key observation or assessment on the matter is wrong. At the time of Long's research, the documents were jumbled loosely in four folders. About a decade later, the society put all the records on microfilm more or less in chronological order. This step made analysis much easier and promotes accuracy.

A lawyer advised Percival to invest the total award in a Massachusetts Hospital Life Insurance Company policy. Again, Long believed the award amounted to $12,862 and assumed it was placed with the Hospital Life company. Instead, after administrative and legal costs and immediate payments, Percival invested the entire balance of $8,201.47 in a trust within the Phoenix Bank of Charlestown. Long's incorrect assumptions led to his wrong conclusion.

Cummings and Ransom received all of their relatively small awards at the outset. Within a month, Percival began making and documenting income payments to the other four. Almost as soon, the men tried to get all or part of their principal shares. Mary Roache, the guardian sister of Thompson, told Percival she needed $200 because their situation was dire "with every thing going out and nothing coming in."[75] Percival did not budge since in the preceding two months Thompson had received $120 from the trust.

Percival thought that reason enough to deny another advance. Watching out for every penny, in his reply, "Mad Jack" admonished Mrs. Roache: "When you write me again, pay the postage."[76]

By 1840, the trust had almost run its course. Murdock, interested in buying land, convinced Percival to settle and close his account. Howell died in a Boston boardinghouse, and Percival paid his balance of $1,071.99 to his executor. White had only $300.82 left in his account, so Percival turned the full amount over to him and, of course, obtained the usual receipt. Thompson died late in the year, and his remaining amount of $800 went to his executors. The trust could be closed.

Percival gathered up all of the trust documents in his possession and secured them under a cover sheet reading, "The accts of Thos Murdock, James Thompson, Joshua Howell, and Charles W White settled & signed & sealed, thank God—J Percival." This bulky file conclusively demonstrates every penny of the awards went to the beneficiaries, their executors or legitimate administrative costs, and Percival administered the trust honestly, fairly and prudently.

After his deficient review of the trust file, Long jumped to Percival's will and noted the Executor's Inventory listed "cash deposited in the Mass. Hospital Insurance Co. & due on the policy no. 3196—$12,781.10." Aha, thought Long. "This is surely close enough"[77] to the incorrect amount he wrongly believed was entrusted to the Hospital Insurance company. It must be the trust money. Percival stole it.

So, insufficient research meant Long did not gather information necessary to reach an accurate conclusion. Moreover, he did not correctly analyze the information he had gathered. When Long concluded that Percival made off with all of the trust funds, he did not first ask himself, "Am I sure?"

Now that "Mad Jack" has been taken care of, it seems fitting to move on to the Wicked Witch of the West.

CHAPTER 5

TOO GOOD TO BE TRUE

As discussed, whenever an organization claims a notable first, the matter just begs for scrutiny. When the entity is in the storytelling business, the claim somehow seems all the more suspicious. The Cape Cinema located in Dennis, one of the top cultural spots on Cape Cod, is involved in such a situation. While admitting it is "difficult for many to believe," for years, the cinema has advertised itself as the theater that alone hosted the world premiere of the classic film *Wizard of Oz*.[78] While harmless and fun, the boast does not match the facts.

As so often is the case, organizations that go a little too far embellishing their story give the appearance of neglecting what is noteworthy about themselves. This certainly is the case with the Cape Cinema. A purported screening of a world premiere is insignificant compared to what is remarkable about the place.

Raymond Moore had enjoyed success with his contiguous Cape Playhouse. Mrs. Hayden Richardson of the Sign of the Motor Car Inn had urged him to leave Provincetown and create a theater in the village. Moore accepted the idea and purchased the closed and deteriorating Nobscussett meetinghouse for the purpose. Mr. I. Grafton Howes cut the old building in half, pulled away one end and filled it in with new construction. The Playhouse opened in 1927 and enjoyed immediate and great success. Moore was not finished. He had in mind an arts complex and proceeded to buy up twenty-seven acres for expansion. A movie theater or cinema became the next piece of the overall plan.

Mrs. Edna Tweeny joined Moore in putting up the Cape Cinema, a $150,000 construction project that led to an opening on July 1, 1930. Architects Alfred Easton Poor and Robert Pliny Rogers of New York designed the new structure with a front patterned after the South Congregational Church some fourteen miles to the west in Centerville. From time to time, this has prompted some movie patrons to wonder when the place last served as a church. But what is inside is much more important.

A 6,400-square-foot canvas mural designed by famed artist Rockwell Kent graces the elliptical vaulted ceiling. Titled *The Heavens*, the soaring mural in blues, golds and oranges is widely considered Kent's greatest work. "The Milky Way, comets, galaxies and constellations, the Dog Star and the Bull are all there, while floating through this imaginary, imaginative firmament are pairs of embracing lovers and free-flying individuals who seem to be on their own personal space odysseys. The whole effect is one of vast space, grandeur, color, and beauty."[79] Over twice the size of Tintoretto's *Paradise*, it is said to be the world's largest single canvas.

Rockwell Kent (1882–1971) was a preeminent American painter, writer and adventurer. Considered a transcendentalist by some, he read Emerson and Thoreau and had an affinity for the wilderness. At various times, he lived in northern latitudes such as Alaska, Newfoundland, Greenland, Minnesota, Vermont and on Maine's Monhegan Island, where clear night skies may have influenced the concept of his Dennis mural. A political activist, with radical viewpoints, he did most of his part of the project in New York because, as he said, "following the murder of Sacco and Vanzetti, I had sworn never again to have anything to do with—and that, to me meant not to do anything in— the Commonwealth of Massachusetts."[80]

The actual painting was done on the stage of a New York theater on strips of canvas by Kent's collaborator, theatrical designer Jo Mielziner. Carried to the Cape, the strips were then glued to the cinema ceiling. In the end, Kent showed up in Dennis for a few days to supervise the final steps and later returned to autograph the work. Fifty years later, the mural had deteriorated due to roof leaks and being in an unheated building. A complete restoration took place in late 1981.

This art treasure far surpasses any number of world premieres. So, what about *The Wizard of Oz*?

The movie is rightfully considered among the best-loved films ever made. Based on L. Frank Baum's 1900 book *The Wonderful Wizard of Oz*, the making of the movie presents an interesting history. The Cape Cinema became involved through actress Margaret Hamilton, who played the Wicked

Left: Cape Cinema, Dennis, Massachusetts. *J.H. Ellis.*

Below: *Wizard of Oz* poster. *Private collection.*

Witch of the West character. She was at the playhouse as the release date approached and obtained a test or prerelease showing for the cinema. The concept of the film traces to 1933 and the success of Paramount's *Alice in Wonderland* movie. The following success of *Snow White and the Seven Dwarfs* in 1937 intensified interest. 20th Century Fox thought of acquiring the screen rights and planned to feature Shirley Temple in the production. MGM did secure the rights and put Judy Garland in the lead role of Dorothy. A series of writers came and went, and the plot underwent several modifications. Various actors and actresses were considered. Edna Mae Oliver was an early choice for the Wicked Witch role, as was Gale Sondergaard before Hamilton got the nod.

In addition to staff and plot changes, there were accidents and illnesses that hampered the production. Hamilton suffered first-degree burns on her face as well as lesser burns on her hands when exiting through smoke and flames during the Munchkinland scene. She missed two months of work.

On Friday night, August 11, 1939, the movie showed in Dennis with fanfare and many Hollywood and stage personalities in the audience. Attendees included Sally Eilers and Otto Preminger of 20th Century Fox and Glenda Farrell and Douglas Montgomery of Warner Bros. Nearby summer resident and star of Broadway Gertrude Lawrence joined the festivities. At the time, it was understood that on the same evening, Oconomowoc, Appleton and Oshkosh, Wisconsin, would serve as test markets, and the movie would show in those communities on the same night. From this, it was incorrectly presumed the film rolled first in Dennis because it was in an earlier time zone.

For some reason, Oconomowoc for years also celebrated as the one place where the movie debuted. A Milwaukee newspaper dug into the topic and concluded, "Oconomowoc doesn't hold the title."[81] The American Film Institute, referencing the *Green Bay Press-Gazette*, indicates the first showing took place in that city's Orpheum Theatre on August 10, 1939—the day before Dennis. Therefore, Dennis and the three other Wisconsin communities fell to second place. Originally, the world premiere was scheduled for the Cathay Circle Theatre in Los Angeles on August 9. This showing was delayed for several days and moved to Grauman's Chinese Theatre. The official release took place at that theater on August 15.

Another questionable assumption similar to the cinema caper played into the spreading of an incorrect version of history involving Cape Cod and the War of 1812.

The War of 1812 against Great Britain had a more direct impact on Cape Cod than any other war in the country's history. The British occupied Provincetown. They attacked Orleans and bombarded Falmouth. The Royal Navy lobbed cannonballs into Barnstable and Sandwich, while threatening fishermen and coasters all along the shore. Seeking a profit, the enemy demanded and received tidy ransoms from Brewster, Eastham, Dennis and Yarmouth.

In what was an offshoot of the Napoleonic Wars sweeping Europe, the United States declared war on Great Britain in June 1812. The primary reason involved continued British harassment of America's shipping, including the impressment of its seamen. To protect the country's merchantmen, President Thomas Jefferson placed an embargo on the fleet, prohibiting it from leaving port. Later, the British imposed their own embargo, and their navy dominated the coast. The relatively small U.S. Navy enjoyed some success but was unable to throw off its mighty antagonist. The economy collapsed as a result. Unemployment soared, banks failed and poorhouses filled.

Political division prevailed. Barnstable, Falmouth, Sandwich and Orleans supported the war and resisted the enemy. The other Cape towns attempted to remain free of the conflict. But it was not an easy task. A tender from the HMS *Nymphe*, 38, roamed Nantucket Sound bent on plunder. Master's Mate Charles Goullet skippered the tender.

Goullet captured some coasters off the entrance of Bass River and demanded the towns of Dennis and Yarmouth pay $1,000 in ransom. He emphasized he was prepared to burn five fishing vessels at anchor in the mouth of the river. The towns could only raise and deliver $660. The Brit decided to take it and move south, where he captured a number of Nantucket fishing boats. Some islanders became aroused and considered an armed response. Quaker Obidiah Mitchell took matters in his own hands. He sent a note to Goullet explaining, "We are of the people called Quakers and of the description of Pease makers and have not at any period been enemies to Great Britain....In consequence we feel emboldened to solicit lenity" since "the most correct part of the inhabitance are solicitous and ever have been for Pease with G. Britain."[82]

Not at a loss for words, Goullet picked up his pen and replied, "I forthwith acquaint thee that I am of the description of pease breakers called Sailors, and being at the present time in extreme want of materials to supply my calling, I must pray and beseech thee Obidiah, immediately to cause to be sent unto this, my sloop, at sea four bushels of the said pease,

HMS *Spencer*, "Terror of the Bay." *Private collection.*

of the colour usually denominated green." He stressed, "I trust thou will let the Milk of Human Kindness flow freely."[83] The islanders caved, and Goullet "carried away several thousand dollars of specie, besides sundry other articles."[84]

Towns bordering Cape Cod Bay had much more to contend with than an annoying lone tender. The Royal Navy maintained a forward base at Provincetown. From there, Captain Richard Raggett in the third-rate ship of the line HMS *Spencer*, 74, known as the "Terror of the Bay," went looking for money. He began by threatening to destroy the Eastham saltworks if the town did not pay a $1,200 ransom. Eastham officials did not think long and made the payment. This seemed easy enough, so Raggett moved along to Brewster. He sent a letter to the town's selectmen suggesting the modest sum of $4,000 as a contribution to guarantee the safety of the town's saltworks. Over several days, Brewster attempted to organize an armed defense while trying to negotiate for a lesser ransom payment. Unsuccessful on both fronts, the town paid up.

Raggett also had his eyes on Barnstable. He realized his large ship of 1,917 tons burthen could not navigate the tricky Barnstable Harbor, so he sent the *Nymphe*. An officer came ashore to parley. He threatened to destroy the village and claimed 500 Royal Marines "with seven cannon mounted on traveling carriages" were prepared to attack.[85] Barnstable not only rejected the deal but also insulted the officer in the process. In anticipation of the need, the town had sent to Boston for four cast-iron cannons. The town alerted 1,500 militiamen and prepared to repel an attack. In the end, from out in the bay, the *Nymphe* hurled a shot into the village and, giving up, moved away.

Falmouth was not as fortunate. The town's belligerence upset the Royal Navy anchored in nearby Tarpaulin Cove on Naushon Island. Three barges from the Cruiser-class brig-sloop HMS *Nimrod*, 18, went after a Nantucket sloop grounded at Woods Hole. The local militia hastened to the scene and poured fire into the barges, killing one seaman, wounding another and sending a ball through the British lieutenant's hat. Captain Nathaniel Mitchell responded by bringing the *Nimrod* to anchor off Falmouth and sending in an officer under a flag of truce. He demanded a Nantucket packet sloop tied up to the town's dock and the militia's pair of brass three-pound cannons. Falmouth dared Mitchell to come and get them.

The British captain replied by giving the town an hour to meet his demands before he would fire on the place. Townspeople hastened to evacuate the sick, elderly and children. When the hour passed, the *Nimrod* poured some

Right: War of 1812 cannon, Barnstable, Massachusetts. *J.H. Ellis.*

Below: Model of HMS *Nimrod*, Falmouth Historical Society. *J.H. Ellis.*

three hundred rounds of thirty-two-pound balls into the town. The sustained barrage did not injure anyone, but thirty buildings suffered damage.

A few weeks later, the *Nimrod*, now under Captain Vincent Newton, backed up by the HMS *Superb*, 74, sent a 220-man raiding party into nearby Wareham. The British torched and destroyed five vessels and damaged another twelve. A cotton factory suffered extensive fire damage from a Cosgrove rocket.

Thereafter, the *Nimrod* went on to join a major assault on Stonington, Connecticut. Captain Sir Thomas Hardy with the *Ramillies*, 74, *Pactolus*, 38, *Dispatch*, 18, and the new *Terror* bomb ship twice attempted to get ashore five barges loaded with troops. Connecticut militia beat back each attempt. For three days, the British fired on the town, while the defenders did their best to respond in kind. By the time the attack ended, the British had hurled an estimated sixty tons of metal on Stonington, set twenty buildings on fire, wounded one defender and killed a goose and a horse. The attackers suffered as many as twenty-one killed. Hardy, a man of exemplary character, considered the raid the most unpleasant mission of his life. He acted under orders from Admiral Alexander Cochrane, commander of British forces in America. Cochrane had ordered his navy to "destroy and lay waste" any "assailable" United States town in retaliation for American destructive raids into Upper Canada.[86]

The war ended in February 1815, and the Royal Navy left the American coast. As for the *Nimrod*, it wrecked in 1827 at Isle Anglesey, Wales. Deemed unsuitable for naval service after repairs, it was sold to a private party who put it in the merchant service. The next time the *Nimrod* received attention around Cape Cod was 1998.

Earlier, the Kendall Whaling Museum obtained a reconnaissance permit to explore for possible artifacts on Great Ledge in Buzzards Bay off Round Hill, Dartmouth. Later, the museum acquired an excavation permit for the spot and recovered, among other things, a carronade marked "1778" and four three-pounder (possibly four-pounder) cannons. Based on a superficial review, the museum wrongly concluded it had found armament discarded by the *Nimrod* in 1814. The record, it seemed, supported the conclusion.

After leaving Wareham in June 1814 while running to Quick's Hole, the *Nimrod* grounded near Nashawena. "Employed an anchor out astern to Heave her off," notes the ship's log. The effort failed, so the captain decided to lighten the ship so as to rise higher in the water and float free. The log continues: "Boat from the *Superb* came to our assistance. Got out several of the Guns and Shot."[87] "Got out" does not mean thrown over the side, as the museum surmised. The guns were lowered into the *Superb* boat and possibly *Nimrod* boats. The crew returned the guns to their positions on deck when the ship moved free and clear. Later in the year, while chasing the East Indiaman *Harmony*, the *Nimrod* purportedly ran aground on Great Ledge. This incident is not reported in the ship's log, and traditional accounts are hazy. It got off by itself with little difficulty.

From this background, the museum seemed to commingle the two events and concluded that in the Great Ledge grounding, the *Nimrod* commander ordered cannons tossed overboard to lighten his ship and rise free. Two clues or sets of facts should have suggested the impossibility of this assumption. The first was at hand. Did the recovered cannons match *Nimrod*'s cannons? The Royal Navy and English maritime sources keep meticulous records on such things. The second indicator requires a basic knowledge of tactics and procedures in the age of sail. The museum would not be expected to have this expertise, but it is not hard to find someone who does.

Widely available sources show the *Nimrod* carried sixteen thirty-two-pound carronades and a pair of six-pound long chase guns. The weight designation refers to the size of shot used. This weaponry is not remotely similar, including in offhand appearance, to the Kendall finds. In simple terms, a carronade has a relatively short, stocky profile compared to the long and slender appearance of a cannon. Kendall's outdated 1778 carronade never would be found on a British man-of-war built in 1812. As for the three-pound or four-pound cannons, as of the beginning of 1815, there were only two cannons of such small sizes in the entire Royal Navy. The HMS *Conquest*, 12, the sole survivor of a class of gun vessel from 1794, carried two four-pounder stern guns.

So, the guns do not match those of the *Nimrod* whatsoever. As for tactics and procedures, there is only one situation in which cannons would be pitched over the side. On the other hand, there are other ways to lighten a ship without casting away defensive capability. The war in Cape waters offers examples of each.

A warship would have to be in mortal danger before its commander would have cannons thrown overboard. Aboard the HMS *Belvidera*, 36, Captain Richard Byron found himself in just such a predicament on June 23, 1812. When word of the June 20 declaration of war reached New York the next day, Commodore John Rodgers moved swiftly. In his flagship *President*, 44, joined by the *United States*, 44, Captain Stephen Decatur; the *Congress*, 36, Captain John Smith; the *Hornet*, 18, Master Commandant James Lawrence;

and the *Argus*, 16, Master Commandant Arthur Sinclair, he raced out to sea. He hoped to interdict Royal Navy vessels unaware of the declaration.

Well to the east of New Jersey, Rodgers spotted a British man-of-war—the *Belvidera*. The five American ships gave chase as the Briton raced to the northeast and the safety of the Royal Navy's Halifax, Nova Scotia base. Some forty-eight miles east of Nantucket Shoals, the *President*, out in front, fired its bow chase guns—the first shots of the War of 1812. Byron returned the compliment with his stern guns.

At one point, the *President* moved within pistol shot of its quarry before the *Belvidera* got lucky. "[O]ne of the Presidents chase guns burst and killed and wounded" sixteen Americans.[88] Then Byron "commenced lightening his Ship by throwing overboard all his boats, waiste, anchors &tc &tc."[89] Niles "supposed most" of *Belvidera*'s guns were pitched into the sea.[90] The extreme tactic worked. The *Belvidera* steadily moved beyond the range of *President*'s guns. Within another five hours, it sailed three miles ahead of the pursuing Americans and, before long, reached the security of Halifax.

There are less extreme ways to lighten a grounded ship. A good example took place off Sandy Neck in Barnstable in December 1814. Present area boaters are quite familiar with the sandbar at the entrance to the harbor that stopped the HMS *Newcastle*, 60, Captain Sir George Stuart. Lieutenant Frederick Marryat, on board, later a writer popular in America, was not surprised. He noted Stuart "had been many years at sea, but strange to say, knew nothing, literally nothing, of his profession."[91] At any rate, Stuart offloaded boats, spare tackle, equipment and spars. The crew made a raft of some spars to deploy a set of spring anchors. At high tide, the men hove the ship off with ease. This standard technique could have been employed by the *Nimrod*, if necessary, at Great Ledge.

Incidentally, the episode led to the Battle of Orleans. Some of the spare masts and spars rafted to lighten the *Newcastle* got away and drifted east to that Lower Cape town. Locals quickly salvaged the unexpected bounty. Stuart was not amused. He sent Marryat in four barges on a punitive recovery mission. The Brits cut out a schooner and three sloops, setting two on fire. The militia responded and drove the invaders away, killing one Royal Marine.

Furthermore, demonstrating the nonsense of the Kendall Museum's careless conclusion, a warship dead in the water is not helpless when it comes to dealing with antagonists. Whether becalmed or grounded, such a vessel can be lethal. The war provides a dramatic example and shows again why the *Nimrod* did not have to desperately throw out cannons off Round Hill.

In October 1814, the American schooner-rigged privateer *Prince de Neufchatel*, 17, Captain John Ordronaux, while towing an English prize south of Madequecham on Nantucket, encountered the HMS *Endymion*, 50, Captain Henry Hope. The Brit, enjoying a fresh breeze, closed on the *Prince* when the latter lost the wind. Becalmed, Ordronaux cut off his prize, anchored and prepared for an attack. Once Hope lost the wind, he anchored and sent five boats manned by 111 men after the *Prince* and its 40-man crew.

The British, under Lieutenant Abel Hawkins, placed a boat under each bow of the privateer, one on each side and the other under the stern. The vicious melee that followed is described in the *Prince*'s log: "A warm action was then kept up with muskets, pistols, cutlasses, &tc, and every attempt the enemy made to board he was promptly met and repulsed."[92] The ferocity lasted twenty minutes before the British sought mercy. The *Endymion* lost twenty-eight killed, thirty-seven wounded and twenty-eight taken prisoner. The Americans had seven killed and twenty-four wounded. When Ordronaux made Boston, the merchants presented him with a special sword and a vote of thanks. Years later, in 1942, the navy named destroyer DD-617 after him.

Finally, the *Nimrod* had little to fear by way of a seaborne attack. The U.S. Navy had only seven ships at sea at the time and none operating in the area. The British had almost one hundred men-of-war in North America. The *Superb* stood in sight. While over five hundred American privateers sailed during the war, only several were large enough to hold any chance in a scrap with the *Nimrod*. And none was interested. Privateers tried to stay far away from the Royal Navy.

The tale does not end here. Kendall gave a cannon to Falmouth, Stonington and Wareham, towns plagued by the *Nimrod*. The Falmouth Historical Society received its cannon in November 1999 and put it on display, boasting the British could not get our cannons, but we got one of theirs. Efforts to preserve the piece commenced. Since the gun had been in the salt water of Buzzards Bay presumably for 185 years, it could not be kept in the open and oxygen-rich air. Such an environment would accelerate corrosion. The cannon, therefore, was placed in a fiberglass tank filled with water and chemicals designed to create an alkaline solution with a pH value of 11. The process, over years, would reverse ionization. Unfortunately, the Falmouth effort failed, and its gun is just about destroyed by rust.

Stonington enjoyed more success conserving its cannon but eventually gave up on the project. The Stonington Historical Society employed the services of the Maryland Archaeological Conservation Laboratory to treat its gun. Surfaces were cleaned, and the work found the cannon fully loaded

Falmouth *Nimrod* cannon. *J.H. Ellis.*

Stonington *Nimrod* cannon. *J.H. Ellis.*

with two cannonballs backed by black powder. A fairly technical process of chloride extraction and electrolyte bathing proceeded. More mechanical cleaning, Rustoleum painting and micro-crystalline and polyethylene waxing followed. Nonetheless, in the end, the cannon is considered soft and fragile. Thus, it could not be exhibited outside. As it weighs 1,800 pounds, the piece proved too cumbersome to be displayed inside. Prodded by doubts of its *Nimrod* connection, the Stonington society decided to give up the cannon to its Falmouth counterpart. The two guns—the deteriorating Falmouth one and the preserved Stonington cannon—are on display in a gun shed at the Falmouth Historical Society's grounds.

From the outset, the Falmouth Historical Society advertised its cannon as a *Nimrod* relic. After several skeptics raised questions about such a connection, the society began to back away from the claim. Even so, the group's website continues to tell the story. Moreover, other sites, such as History of Massachusetts Blog, Massmoments and the New England Historical Society, still repeat the myth. Once a fictious claim is advanced by a respectable organization, it is difficult to turn back. This is especially the case when the story seems too good to be true. There is a tendency for the fable to persist as part of the region's lore.

CHAPTER 6

COLORING SPORTS

nverified information can lead to erroneous conclusions that have a way of persisting. The Cape's sports scene, as one might expect, gets involved in this sort of carelessness. The acclaimed Cape Cod Baseball League presents an example. Beginning in the 1960s and continuing up to recent years, it was said the league formed in 1885. A poster in the National Baseball Hall of Fame apparently prompted the claim. The handbill advertised a July 4, 1885 "match" between clubs from Barnstable and Sandwich. This seemed like it must have been the beginning. The league went with the 1885 date.

For years, league and team literature advanced the claim. To illustrate, the league's 1977 brochure said the league "Has a long and proud history dating back to 1885." The Orleans Cardinals 1978 reference booklet used identical language. The same can be said of guides put out around this time by other clubs. In 1996, *Yankee* magazine even fell for the line and described the league as the oldest organized amateur league in the country. In a 2010 special thank-you to its sponsors, in the local newspaper, the league described the just completed season as its 126th year. As recently as 2022, the same paper said, "The Cape Cod Baseball League was founded in 1885."[93] The league, in 1985, went all out and celebrated the "anniversary" with a July 13 "Centennial Old-Timers Reunion Game" at Eldredge Park in Orleans. Former Cape League and Chicago Cubs infielder Len Merullo coached the Lower Division team, and Red Sox scout Bill Enos managed the Upper Division squad.

In a 1970 article about the origins of the Boston Red Stockings, David Q. Voigt offered an explanation for the thinking behind baseball centennials. Although they were celebrated "often with questionable historical accuracy," he thought "they function as rites of intensification for restoring baseball's longevity and virility." And he said, "To the historian of sports with a trained suspicion of myth, such celebrations are a challenge to set the record straight." In the case at hand, the record is clear. At best, the Cape Cod Baseball League can cite 1923 as the year of its beginning, even though much Cape baseball was played well beforehand.

For the record, Barnstable's newspaper reported its team won the 1885 game by a 13 to 2 score, bragging: "No detailed account is necessary."[94] Rivalries had developed over the previous two decades. In fact, the game was the twelfth annual Fourth of July match between the two towns.

Competitive baseball appeared on the Cape after the Civil War. Soldiers passed the time in army camps playing the new sport and returned home with an enthusiasm for the game. Early newspaper accounts claim the first contest in the area took place in Sandwich on a cold November 1865 day. Late fall and even winter games became common. The game exerted such a hold on young men that in the 1870s, they played baseball on Sandwich's frozen Mill Pond, every player on skates.

In June 1866, the first organized team formed in Sandwich. Known as the Nichols Club, it took its name from sea captain Edward Nichols, who let the men play in his pasture on the northwest side of School Street. Soon, other villages put up their own teams. After several weeks of informal play, the Cummaquid Club of Barnstable formally organized in September 1867, as did the Mattakeesetts of Yarmouth. The Cummaquids got off to a great start. In an early game played on a neutral field in West Barnstable, they whipped the highly regarded Nichols Club by a 25–19 score. The local weekly reported the game "was one of the most exciting and interesting which has been played in the County and was witnessed by a large number of persons." The paper concluded the two teams "would…do honor to the best organized club, not excepting the Atlantics, of Brooklyn."[95] (Organized in 1855, the Atlantics, with an 11-1 record in 1859, were considered the first national champions.) The game drew widespread interest since the Cummaquid win over the Nichols team two weeks earlier may have been the first intertown game on the Cape. In October, the Cummaquids ventured off-Cape to play the Middleboro Monitors. Earning a 36–30 victory over a strong opponent, they were cheered by the rival Nichols Club when their returning train stopped at the Sandwich depot.

Sandwich Twilight League jersey, circa 1939. *Private collection.*

Cape baseball continued to grow in popularity. As early as 1867, teams began competing in autumn's annual Cattle Show and Fair. In that year, Barnstable's Cummaquid Club beat the Mattakeesetts 30 to 13 and walked off with the prize— "a beautiful silver mounted carved black walnut bat costing $15."[96] Baseball at the county fair became an annual tradition. In some years, the game featured high school teams. Off-Cape teams also appeared. In 1920, a Plymouth nine took on Falmouth. The next year, the fair held a Cape baseball tournament. Falmouth advanced by defeating Chatham, only to lose the Cape Cod baseball championship to Osterville. Time had come for a formal Cape Cod baseball league.

Attempts to establish such a permanent league began in 1910. Managers of clubs from Chatham, Sagamore, Sandwich and Wellfleet met in the spring and drew up articles of agreement. They scheduled games for Saturdays and holidays since a number of players worked weekdays at Sagamore's Keith Car Works. The Sandwich newspaper reported: "This is the first league outside of school leagues ever formed on the Cape."[97]

The league concept sputtered along. Teams joined and left. The makeup varied from year to year. In 1913, Falmouth Heights, Osterville, Pocasset, South Yarmouth and Sandwich fielded teams. A year later, Falmouth, Wareham, Sandwich, Orleans, Harwich and Hyannis were members. The instability continued. By 1916, only Falmouth, Oak Bluffs, Woods Hole and Hyannis were entered. A year later, World War I put a damper on this early attempt to build a baseball league.

In the absence of a unifying structure, baseball continued. However, the problem of funding persisted. In 1918, Falmouth had difficulty supporting a team, so the town combined with Oak Bluffs. When playing in Falmouth, the team wore Falmouth outfits. When on the Vineyard, the players donned Oak Bluffs uniforms. Hyannis found it necessary to charge admission, selling tickets "for $2 transferrable and ladies…admitted to the grandstand free."[98] Despite operational challenges, the game remained popular. Towns, high schools and businesses fielded teams. Noteworthy in this period, in 1919, Harold "Pie" Traynor of Framingham played shortstop for Falmouth. The next year, he moved to the Pittsburgh Pirates and began a stellar major-league career leading to membership in the National Baseball Hall of Fame.

Tapping into the continued fervor for the game, in 1923, community leaders established a new Cape Cod Baseball League. The group named William Lovell of Hyannis president. Harry B. Albro, then of Falmouth; J. Hubert Shepard of Chatham; and Arthur R. Ayer from Osterville rounded out the board. At first, the league consisted of teams from those four places. As the years passed, other towns entered while some would drop out. The composition of the league varied from year to year. The organization lasted into 1940. Before that summer ended, the league shut down "because of lack of necessary funds."[99] The present league, after seemingly disregarding the 1885 tradition, now traces its origins to this operation that stretched over two decades.

The caliber of play proved excellent. Rosters included some of the best amateur and semi-pro players in the region. John "Blondy" Ryan of Lynn played for Orleans before moving to the New York Giants. Robert "Red" Rolfe from Penacook, New Hampshire, and Dartmouth College also competed with Orleans prior to starring for the New York Yankees. There were others who made the jump to the Majors, including local favorite Daniel "Danny" MacFayden of Truro. He played for Osterville and Falmouth before a seventeen-year major-league career including stints twirling for the Red Sox and Boston Braves. Many college players made their way to the Cape league. Chatham, for instance, at one point was pretty much a Boston College team.

To meet the high local interest in baseball, lesser leagues appeared. A County Twilight League, a Lower Cape League and a Hyannis Industrial League came on the scene before World War II. The Town of Barnstable supported four Twilight entries: Hyannis, Osterville, Cotuit and West Barnstable. The 1940 town meeting appropriated $300 to be split among the four teams. As well, wholly independent teams existed at the time. All of this came to an end with the onset of the war.

In 1946, after the war, elements of the old Twilight leagues got together as the Cape Cod Athletic Association and formed a union under the well-used Cape Cod Baseball League banner. A primary rule required "all players must be bona fide residents of Cape Cod."[100] There were two divisions—Upper and Lower. The Upper Division started with Sandwich, Bourne, Falmouth, Mashpee and Sagamore. The Lower grouping fielded clubs from Yarmouth, Barnstable, Massachusetts Maritime Academy (then in Hyannis), Chatham, Harwich and Dennis. Over the almost two-decade span of this

Yarmouth Indians warmup jacket letter and logo, 1951. *Private collection.*

attempt at a league, Brewster, Cotuit, Eastham, Orleans, Otis Air Force Base, North Truro Air Force Station and Harwich's Cape Verdean Club entered teams. Teams dropped in and out. The alignment was not fixed.

Soon, the residency rule was relaxed to allow seasonal or summer residents the opportunity to play. Before long, as local interest waned, the residency rule became a dead letter. More and more college players appeared on teams, a sign of things to come. Player quality in this town team era varied greatly. There were a handful of outstanding and skilled players—former or future minor leaguers. The general caliber of the league is best illustrated by the fact that in 1954, the Orleans entry won the Massachusetts State Semi-Pro Tournament, beat Vermont for the New England title and placed seventh in the Nationals in Wichita, Kansas.

Change came in 1963. At the time, New England college players filled most of the rosters. The league took the logical step of gaining the sanction of the National Collegiate Athletic Association. Local newspapers announced the "new Cape Cod Baseball League will open its first season on Saturday, June 15."[101] As the fledgling operation strived to establish itself, advocates began bending the truth. The 1885 myth appeared. More was needed. The league began claiming Hall of Famer "Pie" Traynor as an alum. Traynor, as mentioned, played with Falmouth before any version of a Cape league took hold. League publicity boasted former players "Red" Rolfe and "Mickey" Cochrane also went on to the Hall. The boast was untrue. Rolfe, who played for Orleans, is not in the Hall. And Cochrane, who is in the Hall, never played for any Cape team. Cochrane, out of Bridgewater, used the alias Frank King prior to entering the Majors. He starred in five sports at Boston University and wanted to preserve his amateur status while playing semi-pro ball. He continued using the alias while in the minors, thinking if at first, he failed, he could start fresh using his real name. An exhaustive records search did not uncover a Cochrane or King playing for a Cape club at the time.

The Rolfe and Cochrane untrue claims gradually faded. Over six decades, the current league matured to the point that stretching the truth about past players became superfluous. Highly organized and well managed, it now enjoys an exemplary reputation. Many objective observers consider it the best summer collegiate league in the country. Over one thousand former players have moved up to the Majors. A fair number became All-Stars, while four have made it to the Hall. Carlton Fisk (Orleans), Frank Thomas (Orleans), Craig Biggio (Yarmouth-Dennis) and Jeff Bagwell (Chatham) have received this high honor.

Baseball is not the only Cape sport that struggles to get it correct. The golf scene for years has had difficulty with the adjectives *first* and *oldest*. Depending on the source, three golf courses vie for the honor of being the first on Cape Cod. One of the three no longer exists. Vanished Wayside Links in Yarmouth Port is said by some to be the first in the county. That leaves Highland Links in Truro and the Cummaquid Golf Club in Barnstable to contest for oldest if not first out of some forty courses now on the Cape.

Somewhat surprisingly, a fair number of courses have come and gone. Shawme in Sandwich disappeared without a trace. A "Golf links" existed at the Cotuit Park as early as 1894. No longer remaining, the grounds were "said to be by the professors in the game second to none in the country."[102] Cedar Banks Links in Eastham, also among the lost, enjoyed a great run. Created by Quincy Adams Shaw in 1925–28, the 72-par, eighteen-hole course passed gradually. Cut to nine holes in 1935, it no longer existed by 1960. Nonetheless, it had its day. Legendary Francis Ouimet, 1913 U.S. Open champion, often played the course. Bobby Jones, one of the greatest, in 1931 managed a one-over par 73, the best score anyone ever achieved at Cedar Banks. The course covered now prime real estate around and about Salt Pond and the nearby marsh.

Sepuit Golf Club in Osterville opened in 1896, though construction started earlier. Prior to the Depression, it went bankrupt. E.K. Davis, a man who made a fortune in the aluminum business, saved it for a time. By 1942, it was over. The 1944 hurricane tore up many of the trees about the course, ending hopes of a restoration. Homes now occupy the site. In its day, golf greats like Walter Hagen, winner of eleven professional majors, played the course. Other distinguished guests included U.S. chief justice Charles Evans Hughes.

Another Cape course no longer in existence attracted the attention of noted golf authority and course architect Walter J. Travis. He thought the Great Island course in West Yarmouth "smacks strongly of the real article," resembling the seaside links in Great Britain.[103] In 1882, renowned ornithologist Charles B. Cory bought the island to create a game preserve and restore Point Gammon Light. Soon, he became interested in the

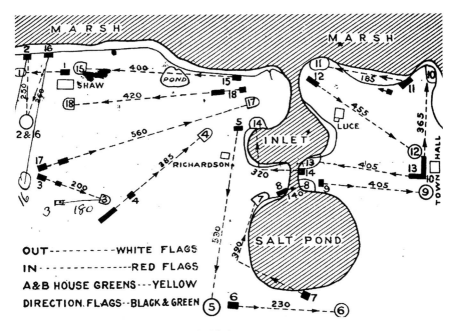

Cedar Banks Links map. *Eastham Historical Society.*

Hyannis baseball team. He bought the players splendid uniforms and strengthened the roster with former major leaguers from the Boston Beaneaters and Providence Grays. Then his interest turned to golf. His first layout included nine holes. In 1905, Cory expanded it to eighteen. Cory lost much in the panic of 1907, forcing him to sell the island. Great Island golfing slowed. A following sale brought it to a close. And when the forty-five-room clubhouse-hotel burned to the ground in 1924, the last vestige of golf on the island disappeared.

The Wayside Links followed a path like Cedar Banks, Sepuit and Great Island. Repeatedly, in publications and on its website, the Historical Society of Old Yarmouth declares Wayside to be the first golf course on Cape Cod, tracing its start date to 1890. The Town of Yarmouth in its 2018 Open Space and Recreation Plan makes the same claim. Two members of the society in a magazine article noted the original owner's family lore sets the beginning as "before 1890, but thus far no documentation has been found."[104] A descendant of the man behind the course in 1998 declared: "It is my best guess that the course was laid out between 1870 and 1880."[105] A history of the nearby Cummaquid course indicates Wayside was "laid out about 1893 or 1894."[106] Henry C. Thatcher built the private family course

An area of Wayside's sixth tee overgrown by native trees. *J.H. Ellis.*

on his estate and farm in the area of Strawberry Lane. The Yarmouth Port post office now fronts the site. The course disappeared gradually. Some holes remained playable into the 1950s. In 1956, Thatcher's heirs gave the remaining fifty-acre parcel to the historical society. Popular walking trails now traverse the lot.

A Wampanoag replica wetu sits close to the spot of Wayside's first hole. *J.H. Ellis.*

Absent documentation, it is impossible to set a start date for Wayside. Best guesses will not do. The preponderance of evidence indicates it was in place by 1894. Thus, as will be shown, it beats Cummaquid by a year. Whether it was the first golf course on the Cape is an open question. Its primary competition comes from Highland, a course with its own uncertain origin.

The beginning for Truro's Highland Links is commonly given as 1892, sometimes circa 1892 and almost as often 1892–98. The reason for the uncertainty is the fact that primary evidence of its date of origin has not been uncovered. Frequently, it is simply described as Cape Cod's oldest golf course. This claim is unsupported, leading the more cautious to describe it as one of the Cape's oldest courses. There is an inference the nine-hole course was conceived in 1892 and completed in 1898. Laid out by Willard Small, son of property owner Isaac Small, the original sand "greens" were converted to grass early in the twentieth century. The spectacular setting in the shadow of Highland or Cape Cod Light and overlooking the expansive Atlantic is rivaled in New England only by the Samoset in Rockport, Maine.

Above: Highland Links, Truro, Massachusetts. *J.H. Ellis*.

Opposite: Golfing in the shadow of Highland Lighthouse. *J.H. Ellis*.

Unlike the uncertainties associated with the start of Wayside and Highland, the beginning of Cummaquid is well known and documented. In 1938, Dr. Gorham Bacon, an original member of Cummaquid, wrote a brief history of the club. Club secretary Joseph B. McLean updated the history in 1959. A group of Wayside golfers in 1895 moved a little west across the town line, bought and rented land, hacked out a course and organized the Cummaquid Golf Club. "It was probably one of the first ten golf clubs to be organized in the United States."[107] Five years later, the club incorporated.

From the above, it can be concluded three courses may have been the first on the Cape. Secondary sources show Wayside and Cotuit Golf Links were operating as early as 1894. Relying solely on tradition, Highland claims a start date of 1892. Supporting data is too limited to tell which of the three set up first. The Highland property is part of the Cape Cod National

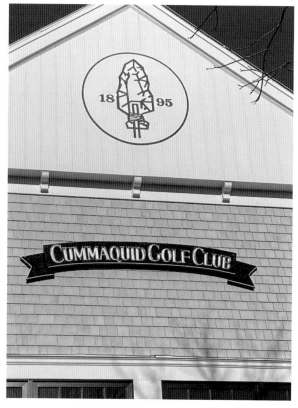

Above: Cummaquid Golf clubhouse. *J.H. Ellis.*

Left: Cummaquid clubhouse sign and logo. *J.H. Ellis.*

Seashore, and it is noteworthy that the National Park Service has not been able to determine just when the course began. The only *first* or *oldest* label that can be applied with any certainty involves Cummaquid. It is fair to conclude the Cummaquid Golf Club was the first Cape club and, of course, remains the oldest club.

By way of conclusion, the first golf course issue is a classic example in mythmaking, and it supports the central theme of this book. An unsupported date or purported evidence is attached to an event, entity or person and repeated over and over until it becomes accepted as fact. This appears to be the case with Wayside and 1890, as well as Highland and 1892. Once again, it is demonstrated that superlatives such as *first* and *oldest* merit fair skepticism. Likewise, boastfulness should raise doubt. Cape history, like history in general, is sprinkled with misinformation. There is much carelessness about truth. And it is just that—carelessness. Deception seldom is a factor.

NOTES

Preface

1. Keohane, "On Embracing History Is Hard Work," 122.
2. Stowe, *Sam Lawson's Oldtown Fireside Stories*, 22.

Chapter 1

3. *Yarmouth Register*, January 19, 1837.
4. *Niles' Weekly Register*, January 28, 1837.
5. Foxwell, letter to Blackington, August 27, 1941, Archives, Camden (ME) Public Library.
6. Ibid.
7. Ellis, letter to Foxwell, August 29, 1941, Archives, Camden (ME) Public Library.
8. Blackington, letter to Foxwell, undated, Archives, Camden (ME) Public Library.
9. Foxwell, letter to Ellis, September 4, 1941, Archives, Camden (ME) Public Library.
10. Ellis, letter to Foxwell, September 25, 1941, Archives, Camden (ME) Public Library.
11. Ellis, "Hole in the Doughnut."
12. Crockett, letter to Foxwell, November 3, 1941, Archives, Camden (ME) Public Library.
13. Ellis, "Hole in the Doughnut."

Chapter 2

14. Myerson, *Collected Works of Ralph Waldo Emerson*, 47.
15. Johnson, *Of Plymouth Plantation*, 243.
16. *Cape Cod Times*, February 29, 2000.
17. Keene, *History of Bourne*, v.
18. Chartier, *Aptucxet Trading Post*, 149.
19. Cummings, "Architecture in Colonial Massachusetts," 112.
20. Ibid.
21. Ibid.
22. Swift, *Cape Cod*, 342.
23. Swift, *Genealogical Notes on Barnstable Families*, vol. 2, 208.
24. Hadley, *Historic Structure Report*, 5.
25. Ibid., 6.
26. Swift, *Genealogical Notes on Barnstable Families*, vol. 2, 209.
27. Exman and Loomis, *Short History of the Sturgis Library*, 1.
28. Williams, *Woman Who Saved a Meetinghouse*, 7.
29. Swift, *Genealogical Notes on Barnstable Families*, vol. 2, 41–42.
30. *Boston Recorder*, January 26, 1838.
31. Barber, *Historical Collection*, 47–48.
32. *Portsmouth Herald*, April 26, 2012. See also *Portsmouth Herald*, February 19, 1944.

Chapter 3

33. Thygsen, *West Barnstable Congregational Church*, 3.
34. Brown, *Pilgrim Fathers of New England*, 29.
35. Dale, *History of English Congregationalism*, 95.
36. Ibid., 30.
37. Brown, *Pilgrim Fathers of New England*, 93.
38. Savage, *History of New England*, 172.
39. Swift, *Cape Cod*, 50.
40. Swift, *Genealogical Notes on Barnstable Families*, vol. 2, 177.
41. *Barnstable Patriot*, July 31, 1866.
42. Mather, *Magnalia Christi Americana*, 213–14.
43. Deane, *History of Scituate*, 169.
44. Ibid.
45. Freeman, *History of Cape Cod*, 244.

46. Holmes, *Chronological History of America*, 311.
47. Goehring, *West Parish Church of Barnstable*, 12.
48. Kittredge, *Cape Cod*, 57.
49. Freeman, *History of Cape Cod*.
50. Ibid.

Chapter 4

51. *Barnstable Patriot*, June 13, 1996.
52. *[Yarmouth] Register*, June 13, 1996.
53. *Barnstable Patriot*, May 10, 1999.
54. Fritz, *Cast for a Revolution*, 72.
55. Hacker, *Minds & Hearts*, 44.
56. Zagarri, *Woman's Dilemma*, 37.
57. Ibid., 38.
58. Richards and Harris, *Mercy Otis Warren Selected Letters*, 15–16.
59. Zagarri, *Woman's Dilemma*, 63.
60. National Archives, to George Washington from Henry Knox, 23 October 1786, founders.archives.gov/documents/Washington/04-04-02-0274.
61. Bowen, *Miracle at Philadelphia*, xvi.
62. Austin, *The Life of Elbridge Gerry*, 43.
63. Zagarri, *Woman's Dilemma*, 121.
64. Evans Early American Imprint Collection, quod.lib.umich.edu/e/evans.
65. Long, "Mad Jack," 118–19.
66. Clark, *Sea Stories of Cape Cod and the Islands*, 246.
67. Chase, *Lemuel Shaw*, 226.
68. Percival, letter to Charles Chauncey, April 18, 1837. Percival Papers, Massachusetts Historical Society.
69. *Wise Journal*, September 22, 1838.
70. Mason Letterbook, October 1844.
71. Stevens, *Isaac Hull and American Frigate Constitution*, 17.
72. *Barnstable Patriot*, October 20, 1863.
73. Melville, *White Jacket*, 36.
74. Hawthorne, *American Notebooks*, 91–92.
75. Roache, letter to Percival, April 24, 1837.
76. Percival, letter to Roache, April 26, 1837.
77. Long, "Mad Jack," 116.

Chapter 5

78. Cape Cinema, capecinema.com/our-history.
79. *[Yarmouth] Register*, August 25, 2005.
80. *Barnstable Patriot*, July 21, 1977.
81. *Milwaukee Journal Sentinel*, August 14, 2019.
82. Whitehill, *New England Blockaded in 1814*, 39.
83. Ibid., 40.
84. Starbuck, *History of Nantucket*, 290.
85. *Niles' Weekly Register*, October 6, 1814.
86. Trumbull, *Defense of Stonington*, 16.
87. Emerson, *Early History of Naushon Island*, 318.
88. Dudley, *Naval War of 1812*, 1:148.
89. Ibid., 156.
90. *Niles' Weekly Register*, September 12, 1812.
91. Pocock, *Captain Marryat*, 69.
92. McManemin, *Privateers of the War of 1812*, 18.

Chapter 6

93. *Cape Cod Times*, July 8, 2022.
94. *Barnstable Patriot*, July 7, 1885.
95. *Barnstable Patriot*, September 3, 1867.
96. *Barnstable Patriot*, October 15, 1867.
97. *Sandwich Observer*, May 3, 1910.
98. *Barnstable Patriot*, July 9, 1917.
99. *Cape Cod Standard-Times*, August 28, 1940.
100. *Barnstable Patriot*, March 28, 1946.
101. *Barnstable Patriot*, May 9, 1963.
102. *Yarmouth Register*, October 27, 1894.
103. Travis, "Seaside Links," 76.
104. Braginton-Smith and Oliver, "Wayside Golf Links," 84.
105. *Barnstable Patriot*, February 26, 1998.
106. *Dennis-Yarmouth Register*, February 6, 1959.
107. Ibid.

BIBLIOGRAPHY

Anthony, Katherine. *First Lady of the Revolution: The Life of Mercy Otis Warren*. Garden City, NY: Doubleday, 1958.

Austin, James T. *The Life of Elbridge Gerry*. Boston: Wells and Lilly, 1829.

Barber, John Warren. *Historical Collection…Relating to the History and Antiquities of Every Town in Massachusetts*. Worcester, MA: Dorr, Howland and Company, 1839.

Bener, Peter. *Meetinghouses of Early New England*. Amherst: University of Massachusetts Press, 2012.

Bowen, Catherine Drinker. *Miracle at Philadelphia*. Boston: Little, Brown and Company, 1966.

Braginton-Smith, Jack, and Duncan Oliver. "Wayside Golf Links." *Cape Cod Life* (July 2004).

Briggs, George W. *Massachusetts Senate Report 2*. Boston, 1849.

Brooks, Paul Q. *The Saga of John Lothrop*. South Yarmouth, MA, n.d.

Brown, Alice. *Mercy Warren*. New York: Charles Scribner's Sons, 1896.

Brown, John. *The Pilgrim Fathers of New England and Their Puritan Successors*. London: The Religious Tract Society, 1906.

Chartier, Craig S. *The Aptucxet Trading Post: Fact, Fiction, and a Study in 20th Century Myth Creation*. Plymouth, MA: Archaeological Rediscovery Project, 2015.

Chase, Frederic Hathaway. *Lemuel Shaw*. Boston: Houghton Mifflin Company, 1918.

Chase, Harry. "A Collision on the Boston and Providence Rail Road at Roxbury, Massachusetts." PDF.

Clark, Admont Gulick. *Sea Stories of Cape Cod and the Islands*. Orleans, MA: Lower Cape Publishing, 2000.

Clarke, Joseph B., et. al. *The Barnstable Conference of Evangelical Congregational Churches*. Yarmouthport, MA: Register Press, 1866.

Cummings, Abbott Lowell. "Architecture in Colonial Massachusetts." Vol. 51. Boston: Colonial Society of Massachusetts, 1979.

Dale, R.W. *History of English Congregationalism*. London: Hodder and Stoughton, 1907.

Deane, Samuel. *History of Scituate, Massachusetts, from Its Settlement to 1831*. Boston: James Loring, 1831.

Dudley, William S., ed. *The Naval War of 1812: A Documentary History*. Washington, D.C.: Department of the Navy, 1985.

Earle, John M. *Massachusetts Senate Report 96*. Boston, 1861.

Ellis, Henry A. "The Hole in the Doughnut." *Pictorial Tales of Cape Cod* (1956).

Emerson, Amelia F. *Early History of Naushon Island*. Boston: Thomas Todd, 1935.

Exman, Eugene, and Lucy Loomis. *A Short History of the Sturgis Library*. Barnstable, MA, 2013.

Freeman, Frederick. *The History of Cape Cod*. Vol. 2. Boston: Geo. C. Rand and Avery, 1862.

Fritz, Jean. *Cast for a Revolution*. Boston: Houghton Mifflin, 1972.

Goehring, Walter R. *The West Parish Church of Barnstable*. West Barnstable, MA: West Parish Memorial Foundation, 1959.

Hacker, Jeffrey H. *Minds & Hearts: The Story of James Otis, Jr. and Mercy Otis Warren*. Amherst, MA: Bright Leaf, 2021.

Hadley, James, et al. *Historic Structure Report: Sturgis Library*. N.p., 2014.

Hamilton, Alexander, et al. *The Federalist or the New Constitution*. New York: Heritage Press, 1945.

Hawthorne, Nathaniel. *The American Notebooks*. Boston: Houghton Mifflin, 1896.

Hills, Leon Clark. *History and Genealogy of the Mayflower Planters*. Baltimore, MD: Clearfield, 2002.

Holmes, Abiel. *A Chronological History of America: From Its Discovery in MCCCCXCII to MDCCCVI*, Vol. 1. Cambridge, MA: W. Hilliard, 1805.

Hudson, Marshall. "The Meetinghouse at Bloody Point." *New Hampshire Magazine* (November 19, 2020).

Huntington, E.B. *A Genealogical Memoir of the Lothrop Family*. Ridgefield, CT: privately published, 1884.

Johnson, Caleb H., ed. *Of Plymouth Plantation*. Xlibris Corporation, 2006.

Keene, Betsey D. *History of Bourne*. Yarmouthport, MA: Charles W. Swift, 1937.

Keohane, Joe. "On Embracing History Is Hard Work." *Yankee* (November/December 2021).

Kittredge, Henry C. *Cape Cod: Its People and Their History*. Boston: Houghton Mifflin Company, 1968.

Long, David F. "Mad Jack." *The Biography of Captain John Percival, USN, 1779–1862*. Westport, CT: Greenwood Press, 1991.

Loomis, Lucy, comp. *John Lothrop in Barnstable*. 2nd ed. Rev. Barnstable, MA: Sturgis Library, 2011.

Lothrop, T.R., and Ruth E. Lothrop, comp. *The Lothrop Genealogy*. N.p.: privately published, 1982.

Lovell, R.A., Jr. *Sandwich: A Cape Cod Town*. N.p.: Town of Sandwich, 1984.

Maclean, J.B. *Cummaquid Golf Club*. N.p., 1958.

Mallary, Peter T. *New England Churches & Meetinghouses*. Secaucus, NJ: Chartwell Books, 1985.

Mather, Cotton. *Magnalia Christi Americana*. Hartford, CT: Silas Andrus, 1820.

McManemin, John A. *Privateers of the War of 1812*. Spring Lake, NJ: Ho-Ko-Kus, 1992.

Melville, Herman. *White Jacket*. Boston: L.C. Page, 1892.

Morison, Samuel Eliot. *The Oxford History of the American People*. New York: Oxford University Press, 1965.

Myerson, Joel, ed. *Collected Works of Ralph Waldo Emerson*. Vol. 8. Cambridge, MA: Harvard University Press, 2010.

Norton, Mary Beth. *Liberty's Daughters*. Boston: Little, Brown and Company, 1980.

Pair, Joyce M., ed. *Women and the Constitutional Symposium Papers*. Atlanta: Carter Center of Emory University, 1990.

Pickering, Frederick M., and John Frink Rowe. *Newington, New Hampshire: A Heritage*. Canaan, NH: Phoenix Publishing, 1987.

Pocock, Tom. *Captain Marryat: Seaman, Writer, and Adventurer*. Mechanicsburg, PA: Stackpole, 2004.

Richards, Jeffrey H. *Mercy Otis Warren*. New York: Twayne Publishers, 1995.

Richards, Jeffrey H., and Sharon M. Harris, comp. *Mercy Otis Warren Selected Letters*. Athens: University of Georgia Press, 2009.

Savage, James, ed. *The History of New England from 1630 to 1649*. Boston: Little, Brown and Company, 1853.

Sinnott, Edmund W. *Meetinghouse & Church in Early New England*. New York: Bonanza Books, 1963.

Starbuck, Alexander. *The History of Nantucket County, Island and Town*. Boston: C.F. Goodspeed, 1924.

Stevens, Benjamin F. *Isaac Hull and American Frigate Constitution*. N.p.: Bostonian Society, 1892.

Stowe, Harriet Beecher. *Sam Lawson's Oldtown Fireside Stories*. Boston: Houghton Mifflin Company, 1881.

Swift, Charles F. *Cape Cod: The Right Arm of Massachusetts*. Yarmouth, MA: Register Press, 1897.

———, ed. *Genealogical Notes on Barnstable Families: Being a Reprint of the Amos Otis Papers*. Vols. 1 and 2. Barnstable, MA: F.B. & F.P. Goss, 1888.

Thygsen, H.E., comp. *The West Barnstable Congregational Church*. Hyannis, MA: F.B. & F.P. Goss, 1892.

Toulmin, Joshua, ed. *The History of the Puritans or Protestant Non-Conformists*. Portsmouth, NH: Charles Ewer, 1816.

Travis, Walter J. "A Seaside Links." *Country Life in America* (November 1904).

Trayser, Donald G., ed. *Barnstable: Three Centuries of a Cape Cod Town*. Hyannis, MA: F.B. & F.P. Goss, 1939.

Trumbull, J. Hammond. *The Defense of Stonington*. Hartford, CT, 1864.

Voigt, David Q. "The Boston Red Stockings: The Birth of Major League Baseball." *New England Quarterly* (December 1970).

Vuilleumier, Marion, et al. *Three Centuries of the Cape Cod County*. Barnstable, MA: Barnstable County, 1985.

Whitehill, Walter M., ed. *New England Blockaded in 1814: The Journal of Henry Edward Napier*. Salem, MA: Peabody Museum, 1939.

Whittier, John Greenleaf. *The Complete Poetical Works of John Greenleaf Whittier*. Boston: Houghton Mifflin Company, 1894.

Williams, J. Harold. *The Woman Who Saved a Meetinghouse*. West Barnstable, MA: West Parish Memorial Foundation, n.d.

Willison, George F. *Saints and Strangers*. New York: Reynard & Hitchcock, 1945.

Zagarri, Rosemarie. *A Woman's Dilemma: Mercy Otis Warren and the American Revolution*. Wheeling, IL: Harlan Davidson, 1995.

INDEX

ABOUT THE AUTHOR

Jennifer Burke.

J ames H. Ellis, a native of West Barnstable, Massachusetts, and descendant of some of the leading first English settlers of Cape Cod, spent a career in government and civic affairs. A U.S. Air Force veteran of the Korean War, he graduated from the Honors College, Michigan State University. He headed the Crime Analysis Unit of the St. Louis, Missouri Police Department and worked as a management consultant for the International Association of Chiefs of Police. Ellis served as a senior staff member of good government organizations in Hartford and Boston and was chief of the Massachusetts State Police planning bureau. Later, he served in management positions with the U.S. Justice, Interior, Treasury and Labor Departments. He is the author of *Mad Jack Percival: Legend of the Old Navy* (2002), *A Ruinous and Unhappy War: New England and the War of 1812* (2009) and *Luminaries of Early West Barnstable: The Stories of a Cape Cod Village* (2014), and he is a regular contributor to regional magazines and newspapers, as well as professional journals.